I0838795

(THE MYSTERY BEHIND THE CURTAINS)

IGWEBUIKE CAMILLUS OKOYE

FIRST PUBLISHED
FEBRUARY 2021

CFELS

PUBLICATIONS

Centre for English Language Studies
118 Tenant Road, Aba, Abia State.

THE FUNDERMENTALS OF
THE HOLY ORACLES 1

08060287009,
08066676113.

© IGWEBUIKE CAMILLUS OKOYE
  +234 803 326 1703, gwebis@yahoo.com

ALL RIGHT RESERVED

No part of this publication may be reproduced in whole or part, or stored in a retrieval system or transmitted in any form or by any means, electronics, mechanical, photocopying, recording or otherwise without the written permission of the copyright owner.

PRINTED AND BOUND IN NIGERIA

De-Kaloo Enterprise

102 Jubilee Road, Aba, Abia State
08060401473, 08052779378
dearkaloo@yahoo.com

DEDICATION

Dedicated to God Almighty, the God of inspiration and revelations.

ACKNOLEDGEMENTS

My Gratitude goes to God Almighty, who owns the inspirations and revelations.

To Finis Jennings DAKE and his Dake's annotated reference Bible.

To the publishers of the "Word Among Us" the publication that has led my daily meditations for circle of years.

To English section of Catholic Biblical Movement of Nigeria, St John Parish Gboko, Benue State. The organization that challenged my scriptural knowledge by making me their Vice President

To Benny Hinns and his message tape titled the Tabernacle and to my Family and friends for their supports and encouragement.

TABLE OF CONTENTS

PART 1

PART 2

PREFACE

The Tabernacle
(Ex. 25-27, 30 and Heb. 9)

And the Lord spake unto Moses saying speak unto the children of Israel, that they bring me an offering of every man that giveth it willingly with his heart ye shall take my offering. And let them make me a Sanctuary, that I may dwell among them. According to all that l shew thee, after the pattern of the Tabernacle, and the pattern of all the instruments thereof, even so shall you make it (Ex. 25:1-2,8-9).

God by revelation shewed Moses a heavenly Tabernacle that has the pattern of what he shall build on earth as a Sanctuary, a dwelling place of God among men. It was a dwelling place of God and a shadow of something deeper than just a building; which can clearly be seen in the light when the above quotation is compared with the message of Isaiah which says:

Sanctify the LORD of hosts himself, and let him be your fear and let him be your dread. And he shall be for a Sanctuary; but for a stone of stumbling and for a rock of offense to both the houses of Israel, for a gin and for a snare to the inhabitants of Jerusalem (Isa. 8:13-14).

The above book of Isaiah explained in a better light the shadow that God commanded Moses to build in the wilderness. God is too big to dwell in a house made of stones, woods and cloths, and as a creator of all things he cannot be fed by man therefore he would not that man should sacrifice animals unto him, His purpose is "Sanctify the LORD of hosts himself" that is to say to men, "Provide a medium for me to dwell with you" or "Make me a channel for me to come down and dwell with you" or prepare for me a holy channel to dwell with you". God himself according to the above book of Isaiah is the Sanctuary, he gave free will to man and would not force himself to man, so he needed a willingly and holy channel to come and dwell among men.

> *Wherefore when he cometh into the world, he saith, sacrifice and offering thou wouldest not, but a body hast thou prepared me* (Heb. 10:5).

God is a spirit, what he asked of man is to prepare a body for him to dwell with them. Regarding God's holiness, it is impossible for him to have or receive human flesh from a sinful man. He cannot also dwell and accomplish his purpose with a flesh that inherited the original sin of Adam. It is a fact that our father Adam sinned and all humanity were yet in his loins, it therefore means that all men inherited sin from Adam who planted men as seed in Eve not from Eve who received the seed planted. God earlier promised to come as a seed of woman alone for man's redemption (Gen 3:15) and such a woman that is willing and holy enough by his grace to bear him.

> *Therefore, the Lord himself shall give you a sign, Behold, a virgin shall conceive, and bear a son, and shall call his name Immanuel* (Isa. 7:14).

Immanuel is interpreted as God dwelling among men (Mtt. 1:23) if the son of this virgin shall be called Immanuel, it means that the Tabernacle was the shadow of that son of a virgin woman and the only son of a virgin ever known in the history of the Jews was Jesus Christ the son of virgin Mary. Jesus came as the reality of the shadow to abolish in his flesh the sacrifices and ordinances of his shadow built in the wilderness by Moses.

> *Blotting out the handwriting of ordinances that was against us, which was contrary to us and took it out of the way nailing it to the cross and having spoiled principalities and powers he made shew of them openly*

> *triumphing over them, on it let no man therefore judge
> you in meat or drink or in respect of an holy day or of the
> new moon or of the Sabbath days which are a shadow of
> things to come but the body is of Christ (Col. 2:14-17).*

The materials used in the Tabernacle were God's free gifts to Israel, from Egypt (Ex. 12:35-36), from the Red Sea (Ex. 14:30) and from their ancestors or ancestral inheritance (Gen. 13:2, 25:5). All these riches of Israel, therefore, were free gifts from God, which God required from their willing heart in building him a Sanctuary, not by force. Now that we have come to the knowledge of its reality it is still on our free will to accept Jesus Christ a rich free gift of God for our redemption which should be given back to God as offering of our peace and redemption.

In the materials used in the building of the Tabernacle as they refer to Jesus the Messiah, we have:

(1)   In Gold, he is Divine, a God

(2)   In Silver, he is our Redeemer

(3)   In Brass he is to Suffer

(4)   In Blue he is a son of God

(5)   In Purple he is our eternal King

(6)   In Scarlet he is our Saviour

(7)   In Fine he is a Perfect man

(8)   In Goat hair he is a Prophet

(9)   In Ram skin dyed red he is a lamb that was slain

(10) In Badger skin he is rejected, he lacks beauty, unattractive

(11) In Shilttim wood he is of incorruptible flesh

(12) In Oil for lamp he is Christ the anointed one

(13) In Spices he is the love of God

(14) In Incense he is Our Priest, our advocate

(15) In Onyx stone he is of the Jews

(16) In Other precious stones he is a light to other Nations

(the Gentiles)

In the first part of this book, we shall collect the materials and the corresponding qualities of the Messiah; Jesus Christ for the Tabernacle. Afterwards, we shall continue in the second part to build the Tabernacle as it corresponds to the Messiah; Jesus Christ.

CHAPTER 1
METALS AND MESSIAH

1:1 Gold = The Divinity of the Messiah (God that Supplanted Man)

Divinity is quality of being God or

like God and this quality was represented

in the Tabernacle with gold and in reality

concerning the Messiah-Jesus Christ, Paul says:

> *Who being in the form of God thought it not robbery*
> *to be equal with God. But made himself of no*
> *reputation, and took upon him the form of a servant,*
> *and was made in the likeness of men* (Phil 2:6-7).

Jesus was God from eternity as St. John in his Gospel also says *In the beginning was the Word, and the Word was with God, and the Word was God. And the Word was made flesh,* **and dwelt among us, (and we beheld his glory, the glory as of the only begotten of the Father,) full of grace and truth** (Jn. 1:1, 14).

For him therefore to appear to the inhabitants of the earth he has to empty himself of such majestic divinity which if he had clung to or retained its essence we wouldn't be able to stand before his splendid essence. He entered space and time in humanity but his divinity is from eternity even as many prophecies prior to his coming stated:

> *But thou Bethlehem Ephratah, though thou be*
> *little among the thousands of Judah, yet out*
> *of thee shall he come forth unto me that is to*
> *be ruler in Israel; whose goings forth have been*
> *from old, from everlasting* (Mic. 5:2)

The above underlined expressed the eternal existence of the Messiah, which means that his coming to the earth does not denote his beginning. He only began on earth in humanity but in his divinity he was ever of old without beginning. David in Psalm 2 reiterated this fact that the divine shall be made human in order to pass through time and thus he said:

> *I will declare the decree: the Lord hath said unto me,*
> *Thou are my son; this day have I begotten thee* (Ps 2:7).

In Christ divinity he has no beginning, was not begotten and was not a son, but in a day "This day" he was begotten, marking the beginning of his human existence, then he became a son. That is why John 3:16 says:

> *God so loved the world, that he gave his only*
> *begotten son, that whosoever believeth in him*
> *should not perish, but have everlasting life.*

If David was not prophesying about the coming Messiah but himself Jesus wouldn't have been called the only begotten son, so if Jesus is the only begotten of the Father we should understand that David was expressing in prophecy the divine made human of the Messiah. The question here is, why should God come and die to set man free? Looking for the answer we found it in the covenant God had with Abraham. Having been informed by God that all the Nations of the earth shall be blessed through his seed, - that is to say that God committed to the seed of Abraham the salvation of the entire creation - God requested that Isaac be sacrificed to Him; The best way of informing Abraham that this salvation of the world cannot be achieved unless by the blood sacrifice of Abraham's innocent and willing son. Isaac demonstrated his willingness but his innocence wouldn't have been enough to achieve a perfect sacrifice for this redemption.

His innocence did not exonerate him from the sin of Adam and no man with Adamic nature was qualified for this sacrifice because with that sin of Adam through which man lost his authority to Satan, he cannot be able to save himself neither was he able to redeem the world. At this point, we are grateful to Abraham who sealed a promise with God in Jacob (Jacob means Supplanter or one who replaced another) when he informed Isaac that God Himself will Jacob (replace) man in the sacrifice. The Bible says:

> *And Isaac spake unto Abraham his father, and said, My father: and he said, Here am I, my son. And he said, Behold the fire and the wood: but where is the lamb for a burnt offering? And Abraham said, My son,* *God will provide himself a lamb for a burnt offering:* *so they went both of them together* (Gen 22: 7-8).

Mark Abraham's words as underlined above, he did not say that God will provide for himself, he said that God will provide himself, there is no 'for' there. Abraham prophesied that God will be a Jacob to man in this sacrifice and God agreed with Abraham to that effect and sealed the covenant in Genesis 22:13 with the blood of a ram. Esau means Completed while Jacob mean Supplanter. When God said and Paul quoted:

> *As it is written, Jacob have I loved, but*
> *Esau have I hated* (Rom 9:13).

It is just as Jesus saying:

> *I say unto you, that likewise joy shall be in heaven over*
> *one sinner that repenteth, more than over ninety and*
> *nine just persons, which need no repentance* (Lk. 15:7).

God didn't expect that man should feel completed either in the atmosphere of the imperfect world or in self-righteousness, he expected that man should understand his need for a Supplanter, the one who will replace him in sacrifice and ransom him for a better atmosphere of eternal joy. Esau and Jacob as God used the names were just an allegory that expressed God's delight in the covenant He established with Abraham in Jacob.

Coming back to the divinity of Jesus Christ, a confirmation was received through John the Baptist when he confirmed Jesus as Jacob God. The Gospel of St John says:

> *The next day John seeth Jesus coming unto*
> *him, and saith, Behold the Lamb of God, which*
> *taketh away the sin of the world* (Jn1:29).
> *And looking upon Jesus as he walked, he saith, Behold the*
> *Lamb of God!* (Jn. 1:36)

He was again confirmed by the Father Almighty Himself in his baptism as Matthew says:

> *And lo a voice from heaven saying. This is my beloved*
> *son; in whom I am well pleased* (Matt. 3:17:5).

During Christ transfiguration also the same claim of divine sonship was laid by God upon Jesus (Mtt 17:5). The Messiah was by his humanity the son of David; David himself beforehand prophesied concerning the divinity of the Messiah saying:

> *The Lord said to my Lord, sit thou art my right hand,*
> *until I make thine enemies thy footstool (Ps. 110:1, Acts*

2:34).

For David calling his son *"My Lord"* it means that he wasn't a son, but an ever existing Lord over humanity. He further expressed in Psalm 102 that the Messiah was the Lord of all creations that even thou he shall come to exist between space and time counted by years he remains divine and eternal, incorruptible and can never wax old.

> ***Of old has thou laid the foundation of the earth and the heavens are the work of thy hands. They shall perish, but thou shalt endure: yea, all of them shall wax old like a garment: as a vesture shalt thou change them, and they shall be changed. But thou art the same, and <u>thy years</u> shall have no end*** (Ps 102:25-27).

"Thy years" is the expression of his entrance into space and time for the salvation of humanity but nevertheless he shall have no end. Jesus as God was the author of all creations, and creations by due time shall wax old but He remains eternal. In the Gospel of Jesus, John confirmed this prophecy as he spoke of Jesus saying:

> ***In the beginning was the word, and the word was with God, and the word was God. The same was in the beginning with God. All things were made by him; and without him was not anything made that was made*** (Jn 1:1-3).

The origin of the word of God was from eternity with God and was God himself through whom all things were created and that word of God was incarnated as the Messiah. Concerning his entrance into space and time in the same John chapter 1 he says:

> ***And the word was made flesh, and dwelt among us (and we beheld his glory, the glory as of the only begotten of the father) full of grace and truth*** (Jn 1:14).

This time and space is what David referred to as *"<u>Thy years</u> shall have no end."* And we know according to the scriptures that the word of God abides forever.

> *But the word of the Lord endureth forever.*
> *And this is the word which by the gospel is*
> *preached unto you* (1 Pet 1:25).

Though he emptied himself to be human yet we beheld his glory, the glory that shows his divine essence, manifesting in great miracles as sign of God among us. In the prophecy of Isaiah concerning the expected Messiah, we read him saying:

> *For unto us a child is born, unto us a son is given and the*
> *government shall be upon his shoulder: and his name*
> *shall be called Wonderful, Counselor, The Mighty God,*
> *The Everlasting Father; The Prince of Peace* (Isa. 9:6).

Looking closely into this prophecy you will realize that there is a double identity of Messiah. In his human origin "a child is born" and in his divine origin "a child is given" in his divine essence he has divine titles and credentials as "Wonderful, Counselor, The Mighty God, The Everlasting Father, The Prince of Peace". It was the expression of these divine credentials that contain in Jesus message to John the Baptist as follows.

> *Go and shew John again those things which you do hear and*
> *see. The blind receive their sight, the lame walk, the lepers*
> *are cleansed and the deaf hear, the dead are raised up and*
> *the poor have the gospel preached to them* (Mtt. 11:4-5).

He communicated to John the Baptist the divine manifestations that define him as wonderful, counselor, father and God, and a Prince of peace, he was doing what no man but God could do and was demonstrating to men the prototype of the salvation he came to give to humanity. The prophet Malachi who foretold the first and the second advent of the Messiah, called him the Lord whom the people seek and the messenger to establish the eternal covenant God promised to establish with his people. Malachi 3:1 was expressing the eternal dwelling of Jesus among God's people in "His temple".

The first forerunner, John the Baptist has ushered him in at the first advent and yet shall he come again "to his temple" to establish his eternal reign over the universe.

Mark the two reference of his divinity in Malachi 3:1

> *Behold, I will send my messenger, and he shall prepare the way before me: and the Lord, whom ye seek, shall suddenly come to his temple, even the messenger of the covenant, whom ye delight in: behold, he shall come, saith the LORD of hosts* (Mal 3:1).

(i) "*The Lord whom ye seek*" (ii) "*to his temple*". It then follows that if the Temple of divine worship; the house of prayer is his, there is no doubt that he is God. As Jesus entered the temple as prophesied by Malachi he also reaffirmed the prophecy by saying: *My house shall be called of all nations the house of prayer, but ye have made it a den of thieves (Mk 11:17)*, fulfilling and reassuring that the prophecy of Malachi was referring to him as the Messiah, the mighty God on His divine assignment towards establishing the new and eternal covenant through becoming Jacob to man in one and eternal sacrifice. In the book of Psalm, David was praising and expressing the eternity of the Messiah's sovereignty over humanity, his divine sovereignty. He spoke of him saying:

> *Thy throne, O God, is for ever and ever; the scepter of thy kingdom is a right scepter. Thou lovest righteousness and hatest wickedness: therefore, God, thy God, hath anointed thee with the oil of gladness above thy fellows* (Ps 45:6-7).

"*Thy throne o God, is forever and ever*" established the fact that though the Messiah in humanity passed through time and space his throne has no beginning and has no end and the scepter of his sovereignty and power is of divine origin. The expression of "therefore God, thy God" shows that the first statement of "Thy throne, O God" was not referring to God the Father. It was the latter that refer to God the Father having anointed the Messiah. The first expression "O God" was referring to Messiah as God with an everlasting throne.

When Jesus say in John 17:5
> *And now, O Father, glorify thou me with*
> *thine own self with the glory which I had*
> *with thee before the world was.*

He was referring to his divinity and eternal throne, the original glory that has no beginning and can never come to an end which is in heaven and shall annex the earth in millennial reign as expressed also by David saying:
> *He shall have dominion also from sea to sea, and*
> *from the river unto the ends of the earth* (Ps 72:8).

Isaiah also says
> *And it shall be said in that day, lo, this is our God;*
> *we have waited for him, and he will save us: this*
> *is the LORD; we have waited for him, we will be*
> *glad and rejoice in his salvation* (Isa. 25:9).

It means that though he has gone back to his divine splendor yet he will enter space and time again in humanity *"In that day"* for total redemption of man and establishment of everlasting covenant. In that day men will recognize him as their God and Lord as expressed above "this is our God" "This is the Lord", the former affirmed his divinity and the latter his eternal sovereignty as human. In another text he says:

> *Behold, the Lord God will come with strong hand,*
> *and his arm shall rule for him, behold, his reward*
> *is with him and his work before him* (Isa 40:10).

The Lord God; the divine Lord; the sovereign God who has come before to start the work of salvation will come again to reward the proceeds of his work. They will stand before him and recognize his Divine sovereignty. In a Jeremiah text, he was referred to as Jehovah Tsidkeenu meaning the Lord our righteousness.
> *In his days Judah shall be saved, and Israel shall dwell*
> *safely: and this is his name whereby he shall be called,*
> *THE LORD OUR RIGHTEOUSNESS* (Jer 23:6).

"In his days" in the space and time of the millennium, he will bring salvation on earth and shall be recognized as divine sovereign Lord and shall be called Jehovah Tsidkeenu. In the oracles of God built by Moses in the wilderness, a sanctuary for God to dwell among men, the first of all material required was Gold the symbol of divinity, the first and original quality of "Emmanuel" God with us. The Messiah whose shadow was given to Moses to express in an oracles called the Tabernacle.

We expanded to come to the knowledge of the divinity of Jesus Christ the Messiah in this topic and in the next under redemption we are going to state clearly according to the philosophy of redemption why there is a need that the Messiah should be divine, why God himself wished to condescend and dwell with man or even die for man. Christ is the junction where divinity and humanity meet for human redemption, that is why the Church affirmed that he is truly God and truly man.

1:2 SILVER = REDEMPTION (SUPPLANTED FOR OUR REDEMPTION)

The philosophy of redemption according to Finis Dakes says

"Redemption" means that one who is capable of redeeming

and taking the place of another or others actually meets the

demands of the law and become a legal substitute by paying

the redemptive price for those who are condemned to death,

because of breaking the law.

In the case of man, Satan caused him to rebel against God and break His law, incurring the death penalty. Man, being under the sentence of death could not pay his own death penalty and also live again to enjoy freedom from sin and carry out the eternal purpose for which he was created. To carry out the eternal plan he had to be redeemed and brought back into full reconciliation with God in order to fulfil the holy and righteous demands of the law and holiness of God. God undertook redemption work for man by sending Jesus Christ to die for man and God raised him from the dead so that the original plan could be realized. This is plainly set forth in the following points on the philosophy of redemption according to Finis Dakes

1. All life, both vegetable and animal is sustained and perpetuated by substitutional suffering and death of innocent victims. God's benevolence, holiness and relationship to the

2. human race made atonement necessary. He had made the race to live forever and carry out His eternal program, so when he sinned it was necessary for Him to uphold and vindicate the moral law and yet redeem eternal man from His enemy. If He had permitted His enemy to escape with this attack on the eternal program He would be defeated in the eyes of all free moral agents who could join the rebellion trying to put God to complete defeat and eternal ruin.

3. Satan had kidnapped man and made him a slave to sin and a subject of eternal death. He held pseudo sovereignty over humanity and for ransom on the principal of possession and consent of a responsible agent or government by consent of the governed. This was the only principle of government that a holy God could establish with the wages of sin as death and eternal life as a reward for obedience. Satan's rights are recognized in Scripture. He is the god and Prince of the world who had power of death and hell before his defeat by atonement (Gen. 3:15, Jn. 10:10, 12:3, 2 Cor. 4:4, Col. 2:14, Heb. 2:14, Rev. 20:10).

4. God decided that through the atonement and the substitution of an innocent victim taking place of

the guilty kidnapped race He would free it from Satan, thus legally and forcefully evicting him, restoring man's dominion so as to carry on the eternal purpose.

5.   The penalty had to be paid for man to go free. If sinful man had paid the penalty, he would remain forever dead. If man was to become reconciled to God again and be restored to his original position, an innocent and a willing substitute had to be found to take his place who could fully meet the demands of the law and represent both God and man. He had to be more than man to be able to live again after the penalty was paid. The only solution was for God to become man and pay the penalty, letting man go free. This way God could be free from all accusations of injustice in forcing another to do what He himself could not do, and His Holy law, justice and form of government would be magnified before all creation in all eternity.

6.   One of the three Divine persons in the Trinity became a man, took the place of man in paying the penalty thus meeting all the demands of God and His holy law and defeating Satan and his hosts (Col. 2:14-17, Heb. 2:14-15, 1 Pet. 2:24).

7.   When Satan put to death the innocent sinless Christ, the court of heaven cancelled all his claims, rights and pseudo-sovereignty over his victims. Now he holds a false authority over them. His chief method now is intimidation. All who assert their legal, redemptive blood bought, and divine rights and resist him can be free from sin, sickness and Satanic powers. All believers are now representatives and officers of God's law and can dispossess and cast out devils. They have the power of attorney to act in Christ's place now on earth (Mk. 16:17-18, Jn 14:12-15; 15:16). All who refuse to do so and submit to Satan through unbelief are out of the divine will and will suffer what they permit Satanic forces to do to them (Eph. 4:27, 6:10-18, Mt. 17:20).

Now real faith proves Satan impotent (Job 4:7, 1 Pet. 5:7-8, 2 Cor. 10:5-7, Eph. 6:10-18). God assumes responsibility for salvation and keeps men free on condition of meeting His terms of repentance and holy living (Lk 13:1-5, Col 2:6-7, Heb. 12:14-15, 1 Jn. 1:7-9 etc). Satan is now only the accuser of the brethren and has no legal claim on them (Rev. 12:10) Christ is their defense attorney (1 Jn. 2:1-2, Rom. 8:33-34). The law must still be upheld and God cannot excuse any sin. No human court can forgive and justify any man who continues to commit crimes. So it is with the court of heaven. The supreme

Judge is sworn to uphold the demands of the law in every case. All sin must be confessed and the life consecrated to obedience to the moral law before one is justified and Satan loses his case in the court of Heaven. If one commits sin and refuses to confess and rectify his life, Satan wins his case and God is under obligation to pass the sentence of the broken law (Num. 14:18, Rom. 1:29-32, 1 Cor. 6:9-11, Gal. 5:19-21, 6:7-8,
Jam. 2:10) Dakes Reference Bible.

Before the coming of Jesus as we know, every life on earth was sustained by the suffering and death of another; millions of animals were sacrificed annually in Israel and many more in all the ends of the earth so that life may be sustained. Some sacrificed to sustain this life and others to sustain eternal life. The reason being that man is destined to death and hell, and Satan has pseudo sovereignty over death and hell, and even over man himself. God for his love on humanity allowed that life and blood of other of his creation be used for atonement of sin and sustenance of life for a while. There is other situation, in Isaiah that says:

> *For I am the Lord thy God, the Holy one of Israel, thy Saviour: I gave Egypt, for thy ransom, Ethiopia and Seba for thee. Since thou was precious in my sight,*

> *thou hast been honourable, and I have loved thee; therefore, will I give men for thee, and people for thy life* (Isa. 43:3-4).

If it was in the power of Satan to destroy all humanity, he would have done that before ever the coming of the Messiah but amidst man's rebellion, the covenant of redemption of God given to man stands sure. In the above Isaiah scripture, we read, the idea there is that it has been ruled in the heavenly court that either Israel or the other nations shall perish. It follows that as long as the wages of sin is death and these nations deserve death because they have sinned, the only option left for God is to make choice of whom to vindicate between Israel and those other nations. He therefore chose to redeem his people Israel and the other countries be destroyed instead.

If the Messiah had not come, one life will always stand as a substitute as to sustain another but by his innocent blood he has taken from Satan the key to death and hell and has abolished all those life substitutions for he has set free the captivities of Satan and with strong faith bestowed on His redemptive blood the power sustain our life unto eternity. Silver being the symbol of redemption shows that the divine that is made human was for our redemption.

1:3 BRASS (BRONZE) = SUFFERING (REDEEMED HUMANITY THROUGH SUFFERING)

Suffering is pain God permits or allows man to pass through as to be refined and be perfect like a metal that is passed through fire is perfect and this is called chastisement. Or pains man agreed by himself to pass through as atonement for his sin as also to be perfect that is called penance. The man God created was permitted by God to enjoy himself eternally in the idyllic and blissful atmosphere of Eden that is void of suffering. The commandment that God gave to man in

Eden against eating of the forbidden fruit in other to remain perfect and continue forever in Eden has a seal of agreement in heaven because man did not oppose his submissiveness to that command.

Man therefore going contrary to that command was a breach of agreement that deprived man of God's eternal purpose of idyllic life. Man therefore ended up in suffering as a consequence of sin. As a breach of agreement, this man's suffering became pains man agreed by himself to pass through as a ransom for his perfection and God was justified to allow man to pass through these pains because man was earlier informed of the consequences of sin and he agreed to that effect. Amidst all the suffering of man, man needed a singleness of purpose that is focused on God as to attain this perfection but because man has enjoyed a lot of idyllic life of food in Eden; the food also that sent him into suffering. The quest of food and idyllic life on earth against God's eternal purpose destroyed man's ability to have singleness of purpose but serve God and his belly at the same time thereby perpetuating rebellion against the Divine and eternal plan of God. Heaven was closed on man and hell opened its mouth emitting more sufferings.

For man to be free from suffering it needed an innocent and a sinless son of man who will suffer agonizingly for the sin of man and atone completely the sinful contradictions of man that brought about suffering thereby vindicating man from suffering (Heb. 12:3). A son of man who will through obedience with singleness of purpose break the curse of disobedience that enshrouded man in suffering, triumph over hell, open the gate of heaven so that God's blessing will descend on the cursed earth. If a man begotten of Adam should try to do it, the sinful nature of Adam would not have permitted him, being subjected to hell because of sin, hell will not permit him to ascend to heaven as to complete this assignment. It therefore needed a man that is not begotten of Adam as to be sinless, a man with sense of direction as to willingly suffer for the sin of man and triumph over it.

In other to vindicate man from suffering and also be free from all blame from any free moral agent, God himself condescended to be born of an innocent woman (Gen. 3:15, Isa. 7:14) void of the sinful nature of Adam as to vindicate man from suffering. One person of The Trinity became a son by the power of the Holy Spirit through a woman (Lk. 1:35, Mtt. 1:20) and took the position of man in suffering and being sinless, the power of hell cannot hold him. He therefore triumphed over suffering and hell, ascended into heaven, opened the gate of heaven and sent the spirit of God to renew the face of the earth.

For these reasons, we shall not suffer with sin again which he suffered to cleanse us from completely (Mtt. 1:21, 2 Cor. 5:17-21). We shall no more suffer from sickness which he died to take away from men (Isa 53; Mtt. 8:16-17, 1 Pet. 2:24, Job 5:14-16). We have been immuned from sickness and were given power to heal others through his suffering and blood shed for us. There shall be no more failure in business and no poverty (Ps. 1:3-4). He has taken away our bad habits by his suffering (Rom 6:14-23, 1 Cor. 6:9-11). We will no more suffer lack of spiritual power (Mtt. 17:20, 1 Cor. 12). And failure in prayer we shall suffer, no more (Rom. 8:26-27). If we yet suffer, we have to look at our priority and set what is wrong right. If our desires we seek are what we will eat, drink and put on the pains of suffering will yet enshroud us but if our aim is God's kingdom and its righteousness. We will receive the Holy Spirit that renews the face of the earth and our suffering will be no more. If your own face of the earth is not renewed, then it is yet cursed and cannot yield its increase for you. And if the curse of disobedience is not broken in you by the anointing of the Holy Spirit you are yet in your suffering.

As we embrace God's will and let go our own, our self-centeredness will diminish, then the life of the Holy Spirit will deepen within us and put to death our self-preoccupation, if we open our hearts to life in spirit, this life will shine forth to the glory of God and bless us

> ***Beloved, I wish above all things that thou mayest prosper and be in health, even as thy soul prospereth*** (3 Jn 2).

It is only the prosperity of the soul that destroys suffering and our soul shall only prosper as we begin to learn in the presence of the Holy Spirit, the wisdom of the Scripture, we begin to surrender to the Lord our dreams and desires, and have rest of mind, otherwise the burdens are too heavy (Mtt. 11:28-30).

We need to have the accurate knowledge of him who vindicated us from suffering before our suffering shall be done away with. It is like in a rich home that suddenly crumbled to poverty and the father of the house sent away everybody to the street to earn living, but there was no job and everybody was languishing in hunger. Fortunately, a brother of the house they had never heard of, came back with a lot of riches and went out on the street looking for his brothers to come back home. If any of his brothers saw him and ignore him because he never knew him before, he shall yet remain in his suffering. If another also listened to him and did not believe him, he shall yet remain in his suffering and some others might have got used to riotous life and had no need to be caged at home any more. This is the kind of problems we have as man, we rejected the invitation of him who ransomed us from our suffering and we remained in our pains.

Brass, the symbolic of suffering was that as man has through sin chose to suffer and die, his redemption shall only be achieved through suffering to death.

CHAPTER TWO
CLOTHES AND
THE MESSIAH

2:1 BLUE LINEN - THE ROYAL SON - THE PRINCE - THE BLUE BLOOD (AS A PRINCE WITH GOD AND MAN SHALL HE PREVAIL THROUGH SUFFERING)

We have emphasized so much under the Gold topic,

the divinity and the divine sonship of the Messiah.
He is a Prince with God and with man, the real owner of the name Israel even as the prophecy goes thus:

> *And he said, Thy name shall be called no more Jacob but Israel, for as a Prince hast thou power with God and with man, and hast prevailed* (Gen 32:28).

The name "Jacob" means a supplanter - one who replaced another -. The covenant God made with man for man's redemption as we discussed under the topic Redemption was in the above Genesis quotation established with Jacob. In the agreement we have the law of double reference established, where God also is to be referred to as Jacob, because he shall be coming to supplant man on earth for man's redemption.

Though God shall condescend on earth to become Jacob to man, in the divine law that gave the Satan the pseudo - sovereignty over man, it is illegal for God to descend from heaven and prevail on earth to redeem man as long as it behooves by the divine law an innocent and a sinless man to sacrifice and prevail to that effect. In order that God will condescend on earth to Jacob man and prevail for him, God himself has to be Israel, meaning a God/man's Prince or a

Prince with both the power of God and of man, thereby making God an innocent man according to the divine laws and for this, no free moral agent will have anything against him or find him wanting.

Concerning again the above quotation, Jacob the father of Israel nation was never a Prince because there was not an earthly kingdom before him wherein he was born to be a royal son, but Jesus being traced from the earthly royal throne of David was to be called the Prince that has power with God and with men. He has the royal power of God's kingdom and another of the kingdom of David (Isa. 49:1-3). He was born to man as the son of man and was given to man by God as the son of God even as Isaiah prophesied beforehand saying:

> *For unto us a child is born, unto us a child is given and the government shall be upon his shoulder and his name shall be called Wonderful, Counselor, The Mighty God, The Everlasting Father, The Prince of Peace* (Isa 9:6).

Jesus is a heavenly Prince, a Prince of peace having all the royal authorities of God's kingdom and was given by God through the royal authority of human kingdom to prevail with God and man, reconciling God and man in enmity so that peace may reign on earth as in heaven. In every covenant or agreement reached between two persons, there must be a theme to the agreement and in this God's covenant the theme is Jacob to Israel in vice versa. God was to Jacob the son of man to the kingdom of God to be prince with God and man was to Jacob the son of God in the kingdom of man to be Prince with man. The Bible says:

> ***But when the fullness of the time was come, God sent forth his son, made of a woman, made under the law. To redeem them that were under the law, that we might receive the adoption of sons*** (Gal 4:4-5).

At the mature time of this agreement God condescended and shared with man in birth and in royal kingdom and man also received from Him the grace of adoption to share in His royal kingdom both therefore Jacobed each other that both might become Israel for God. Through this son of God, son of man exchange, the sentence of the Divine court over men was ransomed and men were redeemed from the pseudo sovereignty of Satan to become princes of God. In the Jacob covenant, we have a double-edged adoption whereby God became a son of man through a woman and through her also he was born to David the royal father. We also saw Joseph the husband of the woman as being a humble man according to the scriptures. Having been informed by the word of God that came to him through God's angel concerning the Messiah under his care, he did not hesitate to adopt the son of God as his son and cared for him.

The Prince of Peace also made angels of men as he gathered his disciples and gave them charge to sort for humble men like Joseph who will not despise the word of God, that they may be adopted into the Royal household of God. Angel is derived from a Greek word meaning messenger, I should therefore not be mistaken because in that context, whoever that is humble and obedient to the word of God and also propagate same to others is a messenger of the Gospel and of God. The Bible in the first chapter of John's gospel referred to the son of God as the word of God and later said that as many as received him to them gave he power to become the sons of God, even to them that believed on his name (Jn. 1:1,12).

Representing the Messiah in the Tabancle of Exodus with blue linen informed us that he is to be a Prince with God and man to bring many sons and daughters into the kingdom of God. He has, therefore, fulfilled his side of the covenant, it is expected of us to key in with him and fulfil ours.

2:2 Purple Linen - The King (When he prevails, he will become king over all creation)

The Divine court has ruled beforehand that if son of man should be Prince with God and with man and prevail for man's redemption, thereby upholding the eternal purpose of God concerning man, that son of man shall receive the sovereignty over the whole universe. That is returning to him the dominion given to man in Eden, which was stolen from him by Satan (Gen 1:28). This dominion stolen from man gave Satan a legal power over a sinful man to put him to death, and hold him in hell without being guilty for that. It takes only Satan putting to death an innocent and sinless man before the court of heaven could be able to find him guilty and once

found guilty he will be stripped off of all his claims, rights

and dominion over man and the man shall be reinstated to his

formal position.

To that son of man that prevailed shall the gate of heaven and everlasting doors be opened for, to be made the King of Glory (Ps 24:7-10) and with the authority he received from heaven he will annex earth and have dominion over the whole universe. The first coming of Christ on earth was as a Prince to prevail; he didn't come as a King but he will come again as a king. This is why he said that his kingdom is not of the world of that era. Concerning the Messiah or the prevailed Prince Daniel, wrote in his book saying:

> *I saw in the night visions, and, behold, one like the son of man came with the clouds of heaven, and came to the Ancient of days, and they brought him near before him. And there was given him dominion, and glory and a kingdom, that all people nations and languages, should serve him: his dominion is an everlasting dominion, which shall not pass away, and his kingdom that which shall not be destroyed (Dan. 7:13- 14).*

The Ancient gate and doors were opened for him to meet with the Ancient of days and receive his authority over creation. Christ was God from origin but when he took the form of man and became a son of both God and man, he was as a son of both the heavenly and earthly King not a king himself but a Prince of peace preaching the kingdom at hand. He did not come to restore the kingdom to man as the Jews were expecting (Act 1:6) he came as a Prince to restore peace, and prevail so that he will go back to heaven to receive the sovereignty of the kingdom of God. In the book of John, he was saying to his disciple:

> *Peace I leave with you, my peace I gave unto you, not as the world giveth, give I unto you. Let not your heart be troubled, neither let it be afraid. Ye have heard how I said unto you; I go away and come again unto you. If you loved me ye would rejoice because I said, I go unto the father for the father is greater than I. and now I have told you before it came to pass, that, when it came to pass, ye might believe. Hereafter I will not talk much with you: for the Prince of this world cometh, and hath nothing in me. But that the world*
>
> *may know that I love the father; and as the father gave me commandment, even as I do. Arise, let us go hence* (Jn. 14:27-31).

As Prince of peace he has an everlasting peace to offer not the kingdom for he was not yet a king but because they lacked knowledge, they were sad because he was leaving them instead of rejoicing that he was going to receive the dominion and the kingdom from the Father, they would have been patriotic and rejoicing instead of being sad.

Again he revealed to them that Satan or the Prince of this world has come to put him to death even when he found out that he was sinless. That though the Satan has no right and claim to put him to death, he still insisted in doing that but as long as it is the step by which he is going to accomplish the will of the Father and restore human dignity. He encouraged them to follow him that he might go and submit himself unto death.

Even on the day of his ascension to heaven he was still emphasizing strongly that he has just accomplished his mission as a Prince not a king to that discussion the Bible says:

> *When they therefore were come together, they asked of him, saying, Lord, wilt thou at this time restore again the kingdom to Israel? And he said unto them, it is not for you to know the times or the seasons, which*

> *the Father hath put in his own power* (Acts 1:8-7).

To most first century Jews, the title "son of God" does not conjure up the images it does for us today. For them "son of God" meant, anointed or chosen one, a favoured member of the people of Israel but when Jesus called himself the "son of man" they saw him as referring himself to Daniel vision of one who was given dominion and glory and kingdom over all people (Mtt. 26:63-64) and what this one conjured up for them was so great that they cannot contain it, therefore they termed it blasphemy and handed him over to the Romans to be crucified.

> *Who for the joy that was set before him endured the*
> *cross, despised of the shame, and it set down at the*
> *right hand of the throne of GOD* (Heb. 12:26).

The Jews acted on ignorance, even his disciples were short sighted to truly recognize him, they all lacked knowledge of the Oracles of God at that point in time. It was only Jesus the heavenly Prince on mission that knew his mission and the end that is beyond human reasoning. The Jew actually (ie Sanhendrins) knew what he was saying but they found him with human conceit not fit to be the son of man, the sovereign king, Daniel spoke about. Well it was the Prince of this world that was the architect of the whole episode playing upon the human conceit of the Jews to reject their king. He endured the cross for the joy of being ushered in through the Ancient gate and doors that have be closed since man sinned, to receive back man's dignity from the Ancient of days and become a king instead of a Prince.

> *Wherefore God also hath highly exalted him and*
> *given him a name which is above every name. That at*
> *the name of Jesus every knee should bow, of things in*
> *heaven, the things in earth and things under earth.*
> *And that every tongue should confess that Jesus Christ*
> *is Lord, to the glory of God the father* (Phil. 2:9-11).

He came to establish Israel as a Prince with God and man, that is why he became Jacob of man. There was no way he could have been Israel without being Jacob and there was no way a king would emanate from him unless he first became Israel; it meant that there was no way the Messiah shall be a prince with God and man as to prevail if he did not first replace or supplant man in the sacrifice. There was no way he would be king until he prevailed as a prince through sacrifice. His kingship was therefore reserved until he might have suffered as a Prince and prevailed.

2:3 Fine (White) Linen - The Perfect man (He shall be born prefect and make salvation perfect through suffering)

For it became him, for whom are all things, and by whom are all things, in bringing many sons unto glory, to make the captain of their salvation perfect through sufferings (Heb. 2:10).

Through the suffering of Jesus, God made him

a perfect leader, one fit to bring men into their

salvation. In another text the Bible says:

Who shall ascend into the hill of the Lord? Or who shall stand in his holy place? He that hath clean hands and a pure heart; who hath not lifted up his soul unto vanity, nor sworn deceitfully. He shall receive the blessing from the Lord, and righteousness from the God of his salvation. This is the generation of them that seek him that seek thy face, O Jacob (Ps. 24:3-6).

The only son of man that can ascend into the hill of the Lord and stand before him in His holy place to receive restoration of human dignity and the dominion Adam lost in Eden shall be a perfect man. David question in the above Bible text was to know who was that man begotten of a man that was capable of being perfect enough to accomplish this mission. David knew that himself and all men are shaped in iniquity and conceived in sin therefore such perfection will not be found in man. (Ps. 51:5, 14:1-3). In the last verse 6 he seemed to have found an answer to his question that it was only Jacob the Messiah who was God that can have such perfection that is required to be a Jacob to man, in whom man shall be privileged by grace to ascend into the hill of the Lord, that is why in that verse 6 the Psalmist says:

This is the generation of them that seek him
that seek thy face, O Jacob (Ps. 24:6).

Why should men seek the face of Jacob if Jacob the psalmist was talking about was their father Jacob, son of Isaac who had died thousands of years ago before the era of the psalmist or are we to say it was an ancestral worship. No, David was not known for such worship, as he would say "O Jacob" he was referring to God the Messiah, the supplanter, our Jacob the saviour.

From verse 7 of the same Psalm 24, the psalmist clarified who he was referring to as Jacob by saying:

Lift up your heads, O ye gates; and be ye lift up,
ye everlasting doors; and the King of glory shall
come in. Who is this King of glory? The LORD
strong and mighty, the LORD mighty in battle.
Lift up your heads, O ye gates; even lift them up, ye
everlasting doors; and the King of glory shall come
in. Who is this King of glory? The LORD of hosts,
he is the King of glory. Selah (Ps. 24:7-10).

There are one or two verses in the Bible that poses a lot of questions, like this saying concerning the Perfect man Jesus:

Though he were a son, yet learned him obedience
by the things which he suffered. And being made
perfect he became the author of eternal salvation
unto all them that obey him (Heb. 5:8-9).

We know that Jesus is a perfect image of God as the Bible say:

In whom we have redemption through his blood, even the

> *forgiveness of sins: Who is the image of the invisible God,
> the firstborn of every creature* (Col. 1:14-15).

Why should the perfect image of God need to be made perfect as we saw in Hebrew 5:8-9 text above. It is like asking why should he who had no sin embrace John's baptism of repentance. Well, it follows that as long as man has by sin chosen to suffer, there is no other means he could attain perfection except through suffering and who ever therefore that shall ransom man shall through suffering attain unto perfection. What it meant therefore, as it was said in his baptism; in order to fulfill all righteousness involved in man's redemption he has to embrace the suffering unto perfection that behooves mankind. This is a legal issue that must be proved beyond a reasonable doubt, the requirement needed to be perfect enough to perfect human race is agonizing suffering and to be a Jacob to man and bring man to perfection that Jacob must tender evidence of an agonizing suffering before the court of heaven will confirm him perfect enough to bring others unto perfection.

We decode from the Bible texts above that Jesus being perfect man and the son of God does not nullify the divine law that   has sentenced man to suffering. It is like someone that is sentenced to serve a jail term, whoever that wish to ransom him must plead guilty of his crime and pass through the same jail term whereby if he escapes the law will find the original criminal to serve that term. That Jesus was made perfect through suffering does not denote that he was not perfect from birth; the white linen in the Tabernacle clothes denote that the reality of the shadow shall be a Perfect man, but in other to fulfill the requirement of the divine law his perfection must be confirm through suffering. If he was not perfect from the beginning even if he passed through all that suffering, he could only perfect himself not men because Satan can never be found guilty by law for passing him through such suffering and death. Before the passion of Christ, Satan maintained his claim over every man that is born in the sinful nature of Adam and with legal right over death and hell unless by God's intervention as the supreme authority.

Before the death and resurrection of Jesus many men of the old have through the grace of God and obedience in suffering attained perfection, people like Abraham, Isaac, Jacob, Job, etc, but Satan was not found guilty for bringing them down to death and hell and even held them captive in hell before Jesus descended to hell to set the captivity of the captive free. Though they were made perfect, they could not be able to bring about their salvation or that of their children. Whoever therefore, that shall be able to do this job must be perfect from the outset to the end. Immediately Jesus perfected his mission, the gates of hell lifted up their heads for him to set the captivity of the captive free and bring many sons unto total salvation and liberation. He ascended to heaven and sent down God's blessings and spiritual gifts to enable us endure suffering and attain perfection and salvation

He destroyed the Adamic cross of suffering unto death and captivity, that we might carry our personal cross and suffer for a while unto blessing. Peter says that the God of all grace who had called us unto his eternal glory by Jesus Christ has ordained it that after we have suffered a while for our personal sin, he will make us perfect, establish, strengthen and encourage us with showers of blessing (1 Pet 5:10). The fine (White) Linen in the Tabernacle is a sign that the Messiah shall be perfect in order to perfect others unto salvation, he had to suffer the agonizing suffering that belonged to Adam he came as his Jacob and triumphed in order to make the ark of our salvation perfect. That is the reason behind the fine (white) linen in the tabernacle to depict Messiah the perfect man. He told his disciples therefore in

Matthew 5:48 saying *"Be ye therefore perfect, even as your Father which is in heaven is perfect"*.

1:4 Scarlet Linen - Saviour (And being made perfect, he became the author of eternal salvation unto all them that obey him – Heb. 5:9)

> *And God blessed them, and God said unto them, be fruitful and multiply, and replenish the earth, and subdue it and have dominion over the fish of the sea, and over the fowl of the air, and over every living thing that moveth upon the earth* (Gen. 1:28).

When God created man, the destiny of a man was to accomplish the above quotation. He was destined as a living soul to work his way through all the phases of life, till imbibing the very breath and soul of his creator as to touch the conscious immortality of Eternal joy. Though he was made in the image of God yet he had phases of life to pass through before he can imbibe the quicken spirit and be like his creator. Man therefore was yet on his journey to the tree of life which needed phases of living in Eden to attain to, when Satan intercepted him and gave him the notion that he can be like God without passing through those phases, and man

being impatient yielded to the deceit of Satan and was ruined

of his destiny.

Having been guilty of divine law, man yielded his authority over to Satan. Satan in turn besieged man and the whole earth having pseudo-sovereignty over the destiny of man, man therefore void of authority went on replenishing the earth with his kind and was not able to subdue or have dominion over creation. It therefore needed another man that had attained the conscious immortality and got a quickened spirit, in order to save the fallen man. Man as it stood at this time have no more incentives of Eden as to attain a quickened spirit. No offspring of Adam could be able to save man. God therefore condescended as a man of quickened spirit to save the besieged fallen man. The Bible says:

> *And so it is written, the first man Adam was made a living soul, the last Adam was made a quickening spirit. Howbeit that was not first which is quickening, but that which is natural; and afterward that which is spiritual. The first man is of the earth, earthly: the second man is the Lord from heaven. As is the earthly, such are they also that are earthly and as is the heavenly, such are they also that are heavenly. And as we have borne the image of the earthly, we shall also bear the image of the heavenly (1 Cor. 15:45-49).*

The first Adam was a living soul and was not able to attain the conscious immortality of God. If Satan had allowed him to attain such consciousness and he had a quickening spirit, he wouldn't have been able to make him fall but as the unfortunate had happened, God could not go back in making sure that man should accomplish his eternal destiny. Left for man alone, there is no way he can accomplish in a fallen nature what he could not be able to accomplish in his upright days full of incentives of Eden.

The Lord from heaven as the second Adam did not come to accomplish the first commandment of replenishing the earth because the first Adam has accomplished that, therefore he needed not to marry and replenish his kind but to have his kind through the offspring of the first Adam. His mission is to accomplish the second commandment of subduing the earth and having dominion over creation, so that men shall be saved eternally. Though he was a quickening spirit, yet that does not give him the complete authority over creation, his complete authority was directly related to his patience and obedience to the Father which was not in the first Adam and was the cause of his down fall. His total control of his pride and appetite brought him to the top. Satan thought that the second Adam was like the first Adam, while he was in the wilderness fasting, Satan asked him why he should be suffering himself for a dominion and a kingdom which he had already taken from man. He encouraged Jesus to eat and bow before him as to have the kingdom without much pain; if possible also, let him tempt God and see that God is deceitful about giving what He promised. He thought that this Adam will be like the first, who John Plougman would say that he chewed the bitter pill which he wouldn't have known to be bitter if he had a sense to swallow it whole in the cup of patience and water.

Satan lured Eve into deciding for herself what was good for her against or independent of God's commandment and the same idea was passed to Adam by Eve and they acted on their free will to the detriment of their eternal destiny. For that destiny to be restored, it needed another Adam who shall be contrary in attitude to the first Adam, a man who would be in total submission to the will of God. It was through this obedience that Jesus destroyed all the plans of the Satan and cast down the power of death that once enshrouded us and became also the author of eternal salvation for all men who will come to God through him.

The scarlet in the Tabernacle material was the symbol of the Saviour who shall come from heaven to save mankind from the besieged earth and its gods. He had overthrown the satanic kingdom and removed his siege upon the earth, he had also received the dominion lost by the first Adam, he would come back to subdue the earth with his offsprings who came to God through him and so shall men fulfil their eternal destiny.

CHAPTER THREE

Animal Produce

and Messiah

3:1 Goat Hair – The Prophet

The Lord thy God will raise up unto thee a prophet from the midst of thee, of thy brethren like unto me, unto him you shall hearken; According to all that thou desirest of the Lord thy God in Horeb in the day of the assembly, saying, Let me not to hear again the voice of the Lord my God, neither let me see this great fire anymore, that I die not. And the Lord said unto me, they have well-spoken that which they have spoken. I will raise them up a prophet among their brethren like unto thee and will put my words in his mouth and he shall speak unto them all that I shall command him (Det. 18:15-18).

This agreement of Jacob God/Jacob man was too strong at Horeb as God condescended to meet with man with all his might, splendor and majesty. He was too strong for a man who is subjected to the fear of death to stand before him. The Israelis preferred not to be Jacobed if the promulgation of the rules of this agreement alone should bring them to their early grave. Then God reasoned with them but he could not go back on his word. The deal is done. The agreement was there already in Jacob and the Jacob agreement must be made known to the Jacob man by the Jacob God. There was no way the promulgation shall be done by a man because the agreement was not between sons of men but between God and man. There was also no way the agreement of Jacob should be fulfilled unless the rules of the agreement are properly read in the hearing, understanding and accurate knowledge of the other party.

Giving the promulgation job to Moses could not fulfil this obligation God was owing to man. He therefore needed a means to fulfil this obligation so that it would be justified of any breach of the agreement on the side of man. Ignorant of the law as said, is not an excuse according to the law of man but God is different. The Bible says:

> *And the times of this ignorance God winked at; but*
> *now commandeth all men everywhere to repent:*
> *Because he hath appointed a day, in the which*
> *he will judge the world in righteousness by that*

> *man whom he hath ordained; whereof he hath*
> *given assurance unto all men, in that he hath*
> *raised him from the dead (Acts 17:30-31).*

In order to deal with the excuse of ignorance God now came down and become a man, a prophet like Moses and a brother of the Israelis by birth. He came with human flesh, without his might and majesty so that man could stand in his presence. His coming was to make know all the rules of the Jacob God/Jacob man agreement to man so that God will be justified of any breach on man's side. The prophet like unto Moses was not going to be like Moses in nature because Moses was a man and of Adamic nature. But the prophet to come was going to be in the nature of God as Jacob God from heaven, He was not to read the rules of the agreement from the table of stone or scroll like Moses and all that sat in the seat of Moses, because he was the Lord of the agreement (Jn. 7:15). The issue of being like Moses was in the prophetic sense of direction in higher dimension. Knowing the promise of God concerning his people, the will of God concerning his people's destiny and how to come about realizing it for them. And also like Moses in the promulgation of the rules of God's covenant with man. He was going to be like Moses who repudiated the pressure of being called the prince of Egypt.

> *By faith Moses when he was come to years refused to be*
> *called the son of Pharaoh's daughter. Choosing rather*
> *to suffer affliction with the people of God, than to enjoy*
> *the pleasures of sin for a season (Heb. 11:24- 26).*

The same way shall he who reign over all creation as God refused to claim equality with God but was willing to be born in the likeness of man and to suffer an agonizing death so that man might be saved.

> *Who, being in the form of God, thought it not robbery to*
> *be equal with God: But made himself of no reputation,*
> *and took upon him the form of a servant, and was*
> *made in the likeness of men: And being found in fashion*

***as a man, he humbled himself, and became obedient
unto death, even the death of the cross*** (Phil. 2:6-8).

Another way, the Jacob Prophet shall be like unto Moses is that he will liberate his people from slavery, teach them the way through the wilderness of suffering and adversity. As Moses introduced the Israelis to physical war, gave them charge to go in and occupy the Promised Land, climb the mount Nebo and leave them to fight in the God's presence of the Tabernacle and inherit their promised land. So also the Messiah; the prophet like unto Moses was to introduce his people to spiritual warfare, give them charge to *"Seek ye the kingdom of God and its righteousness"*, climb into the heavenly mountain of God and leave man in the presence of his
Tabernacle (The Holy Ghost and His Body - The Church) to seek and find the kingdom. Finally, as the two great prophets Moses and Elijah appeared in his transfiguration so shall he fulfil the law and the prophets and when he returned, there shall be a final transfiguration of the entire creation.

The Messiah; the Jacob Prophet was therefore to pass through the same phases of life like Moses in repudiation of princely pressure through pains, humiliation, rejection from chosen ones. Those he came to lead back to Paradise will not have access to the promised kingdom until the Prophet is dead like Moses and ascended. As Moses the earthly prophet ascended the earthly Mountain Nebo likewise shall the heavily prophet ascend the heavenly mountain of God. Finally, as we saw the appearance of the two great prophets of God during his transfiguration so shall he appear for total transfiguration of the entire creation. Rough and animal hair garments were mark of great prophets (2 Kgs. 1:8, 2 Ch. 13:4, Mt.t 3:4). Prophets themselves were divine philosophers, instructors and guides of the Hebrews in piety and virtue. They generally lived, retired, being seen in public mainly when they had some messages of God to deliver. Their habitation and mode of life were plain, simple and consistent. The above Deuteronomy

scriptures' last verse spoke of the Jacob God prophet saying:
And will put my words in his mouth and he shall speak unto them all that I shall command him (Det. 18:18).

Jesus actually lived on earth like a prophet but he was different in the issue of public appearance, because the words of God was readily and ever ready in his mouth and as the Lord of the covenant he was conversant with the rules and ethics of the agreement. He was found and seen always in public speaking with authority he has over the agreement, its rules and etiquettes (Mtt. 7:28-29, 21:23, Jn. 7:25) and the Jews were marveled at his commands and accuracy concerning the covenant.

After Christ's death and resurrection, the Holy Spirit became an instructor and guide of the Christians in piety and virtue. Therefore, all believers assume through the spirit, the power of Christ to prophesy the righteousness of God, foretelling also the future will of God concerning man. A prophet today means Christ gift of discernment and vision. Jesus therefore being symbolized in this Tabernacle with goat hair was as a prophet to propagate and guide men on the rules and ethics of the Jacob God/Jacob man agreement and also usher through the spirit many sons and daughters of men into prophesying for God.

3:2   Badger Skin – Lack of beauty, Rejected. (*a rejected stone, a stumbling block and foundation stone*)

Badger skin is a rough and ugly skin of an animal called

Badger. Badger as an English word means pester, to annoy

someone continually with requests or questions – posing a stumbling block. As Badger skin resists heats and rains it is the strength of a tent even like the foundation or corner stone. The first man Adam was created into a beautiful, idyllic and blissful paradise; because of all these, he was fragile. The heaven concluded that the fragility of Adam was closely related to the idyllic and blissful atmosphere surrounding him; man therefore was driven out of the paradise, cursed along with the earth that man shall lose beauty in suffering and wear out unto death. (Gen. 3:17-19)

It therefore requires a man who will inherit such curse to suffer in the face of total rejection, someone who shall reject the beauty of earthly existence between the space and time of his existence on earth as to bring man back to the beauty of the lost paradise. No natural Adamic man who is prone to fear could be able to do it. We thank God and our father Abraham for the covenant established in Jacob, the same covenant that made God the Jacob and the expected Messiah with badger skin strength to bear upon his flesh all the contradiction man inherited in Adam and triumph over them. That was the reason why great men of God before Christ lived with great expectations for the Messiah and that is also why Jesus says:

> *Your father Abraham rejoiced to see my day:*
> *and he saw it, and was glad* (Jn. 8:56).

And in another text he says:

> *For verily I say unto you, That many prophets and*
> *righteous men have desired to see those things which ye*
> *see, and have not seen them; and to hear those things*
> *which ye hear, and have not heard them* (Matt. 13:17).

Concerning the Jacob God, Isaiah says:

> *For he shall grow up before him as a tender plant,*
> *and as a root out of a dry ground: he hath no form*
> *nor comeliness and when we shall see him there is no*
> *beauty that we should desire him. He is despised and*
> *rejected of men; a man of sorrow and acquainted with*
> *grief: and we hid as it were our faces from him; he was*
> *despised, and we esteemed him not. Surely he hath borne*
> *our grieves, and carried our sorrows yet we did esteem*
> *him stricken, smitten of God, and afflicted. But he was*
> *wounded for our transgressions; he was bruised for*
> *our iniquities: the chastisement of our peace was upon*
> *him, and with his stripes we are healed* (Isa 53:2-5).

There is no man born of Adam who can endure these contradictions, to be born and grow like a tender plant with root out of a dry ground where there is no water, that is abject poverty, a pauper in the highest order. Nobody would like him as friend because he has nothing in man's expectation to offer, no comeliness, no beauty, always suffering, under sorrows and grief but nobody pitied him even as it was for the sake of our sins he was born in such an atmosphere. He was again to suffer an agonizing death for men and even as he was suffering to atone for man's sin completely, the same men was smiting him and humiliating him, accusing him of crime he committed not. Who among the sons of men could bear all these things and yet accomplish his mission. Even the omniscient God knew beforehand that man cannot accomplish this task. God knowing that no frail skin of a fallen man can bear this, whoever that can bear such in his skin must have a Badger skin, to lack beauty and be rough from nature, so that when tested with heat and of suffering and flood of enmity he shall be resistant and stand firm for man's salvation.

> *Therefore, thus saith the Lord God. Behold*
> *I lay in Zion for a sure foundation, he that*
> *belieiveth shall make haste* (Isa. 28:16).

In this part of Jacob agreement, it is for those that are not in a hurry - the badger skins – those who lived patiently and endured heroically every storms and waves of this world, it is them that the Jacob God shall translate into paradise because they have shown the life pattern of the badger skin engraved in them. The Messiah was to be seen by men like a badger, a stumbling block and a disturbance to their lives fulfilling what Isaiah said:

And he shall be for a sanctuary; but for a stone of stumbling and for a rock of offence to both the house *of Israel, for a gin and for a snare to the inhabitants of Jerusalem* (Isa. 8:14).

He lacks comeliness and beauty to owe all the words that proceeds out of his mouth and surprisingly they could not be able to reconcile his wisdom with their human understanding of wisdom. He became a stumbling block they sought to drive him away, even to have him executed. As badger skin was not a beloved skin for men because it is not a beauty to display outside, yet it serves as a roof cover from many that hate him so shall the Messiah by love die to save men that hated him and so become both Jacob and Israel for all Nations. The badger skin of a Christian is fulfilling that part of the spiritual adventure of a Christian that puzzles many *"Love your enemy"*. This statement does not make sense from the world perspective, yet for those who know Christ, they are expression of the existing adventure of the Christian life that will lead a man back to the beauty of the paradise. To be a Christian is to bear the image of him who was willing not only to be born in a stable for us, but to suffer rejection and surrender his life on the cross for us as well. By taking a human nature, he suffered a human death for our sake, we rejected him yet he has broken the grip of evil over us. (Isa 53)

3:3   Ram Skin Dyed Red - A lamb that was slain (Rev 5:6,13-13)

This side of the Jacob agreement for man's redemption was made known by God to Abraham when God requested that Isaac be brought to the hill of Moriah outside the city of Jerusalem for a sacrifice. This agreement was therefore made first with Abraham and was established in Jacob. As Abraham went towards God's request the Bible says:

> ***And Isaac spake unto Abraham his father and said my father, and he said, here am I my son. And he said, behold the fire and wood, but were is the lamb for a burnt offering? And Abraham said, my son God will provide himself a lamb for a burnt offering so they went both of them together (Gen. 27:7-8).***

Abraham prophesied the mind of God concerning the sacrifice of man's redemption. God actually did not want Isaac as a sacrifice but to seek Abraham's obedience and the consent of his seeds - represented in Isaac - to the rules of this covenant and to show him also where the sacrifice shall be made - at that same hill that was later called Golgotha - when the Jacob God shall arrive to offer himself a ransom for men. When the obedience of Abraham was ascertained by God, even the consent of his seeds through Isaac, God sealed this agreement with the shadow of the reality.

And Abraham lifted up his eyes, and looked, and behold behind him a ram caught in a thicket by his horns: and Abraham went and took the ram, and offered him up for a burnt offering in the stead of his son (Gen. 22:13).

The idea of the whole drama, between God and Abraham, was to say that though a blood must be shed for man's redemption, it can never be achieved with the sinful nature of Adam. That it behooves only him God to provide himself a Ram for sacrifice, to express his love for Abraham's obedience and his seeds after him, that the world be blessed through him. As I earlier explained, Abraham's statement in Gen 22:8; was "God will <u>provide himself</u> a lamb for a burnt offering" that is also as I earlier said that God himself will descend to be offered as burnt offering instead of the seed of Abraham, to stand as a ransom instead of Abraham's seeds and the whole world. God himself corrected Abraham's impression concerning the sacrificial lamb. God gave him a ram instead of a lamb to inform him that the Jacob God shall not be sacrificed as a tender lamb as Isaac but as a full grown ram of a man.

The Jacob God shall not be so tender as to be under the will of an earthly father but shall be fully grown enough not to be lured but to willingly walk on his own toward Moriah and offer himself there as sacrifice. He will not be also a loved son of man but the one who will be caught in the thicket of suffering against his will, who no one is interested in rescuing rather the only interested man was the one who wished to sacrifice Him even as Abraham was unto the ram caught in a thicket. When God made known to the children of Israel concerning this section of his agreement with man. He brought the covenant anew in Jacob with lamb sacrifice made by Israelis at the day of the preparation of their redemption from slavery in Egypt, showing that this lamb shall be for the preparation of man's redemption from slavery of sin and Satan. That day the first born of Egyptians were used as ransom for Israeli's redemptions, God demonstrated what he would restitute with His first and only begotten son to be a ransom for the redemption of the entire creation. God commanded them in Egypt saying:

> *Your lamb shall be without blemish, a male of the first year, ye shall take it out from the sheep or from the goats. And ye shall keep it up until the fourteenth day of the same month, and the whole assembly of the congregation of Israel shall like it in the evening* (Ex. 12:5-6).

The Jacob God should be born sinless like a lamb without blemish and be set apart by God that he might grow up without blemish. Though it was called a lamb for sacrifice God commanded that it could be taken from goat which means that the Jews shall not be expecting the Messiah only in the aristocratic house of David or at the hierarchy classes of the Jews Sanhedrin but also from the pauper house of Judah, the rejected and outcast of the people. He will live sanctified among the both house of Israel and in the day of assembly the congregation shall gather together and kill him. This was the command of God to Israel in a shadow concerning the Messiah which they accomplished in Jesus Christ. With Abraham the place of the sacrifice of God was made known to be mount Moriah or Calvary Mountain (both are the same mountain). As the lamb of redemption preparation was sacrificed in Egypt the same was Jesus crucified and buried at the eve of preparation and thus the Bible says:

> *And Jesus cried with a loud voice, and gave up the ghost. And now when the even was come, because it was the preparation, that is, the day before the Sabbath* (Mk. 15:37-42).

The preparation here refers the preparation to the commemoration of the day the house of Israel was set free from Egypt and Jesus died at the same hour of that sacrifice in order to be perfect sacrifice for man's redemption. This is just a glimpse of how Abraham Covenant with God was physically established in Jacob; the physical shadow of the Messiah Jacob reality. Jesus is the only one who could give his life or shed his blood as our ransom for sin and death. Nevertheless, whenever we let the cry of the poor pierce our hearts and move us to action we are giving our lives for the sake of God's people. Whenever we let the spirit's call to holiness and purity move us to repentance we are giving our lives for the sake of the church and its witness to Jesus. Jesus has provided his blood for us but he is not to wash our robes for us (Rev 7:14) labourers work for their pay with their own strength (Phil 2:12) therefore work out your salvation.

CHAPTER FOUR

Land Produce and Messiah

4:1 Shittem Wood – Incorruptible Flesh

The shittem wood was made from acacia tree, a very durable wood that cannot easily decay nor be easily destroyed; referring to the kind of incorruptible flesh the Messiah shall be made of.

Like I said before the first man Adam was created from the earth and was made a living soul and was destined to work his way through some phases of life, until imbibing the very breath and soul of his creator and then touch or attain conscious immortality of eternal joy, but he was not able to imbibe in himself the breath and soul or the quickening spirit of his creator as to quicken his mortal body before he was deceived, he was yet mortal when he was chased out of Eden. Yet a dust and shall go back to dust and his soul to be held captive by Satan.

God that created man to live eternally in paradise did not programme in the creation that the soul of a man shall live in that paradise without a body. It therefore, needed a body that is incorruptible (quickening, ethereal), a body that can go through dust and hell and emerge again triumphantly, it will require a son of man that will enter hell corporal and incorruptible as to set free the souls in captivity. Satan has pseudo-sovereignty to control the soul of a man even to destroy the body of them that belong to him in order to hold the soul in captivity, that is why in his temptation he operates in man's soul to insinuate the soul to vanity so that the body shall respond to that vanity, his dominion over man is in soul rather than in the body and that is why it is rare for him to appear in war to a physical body. He fights to conquer the material body through the soul.

The idea of this section of this Jacob God/Jacob man agreement is that if a son of man shall by any means attain conscious immortality or be quickened in the body to enter the hell corporal and incorruptible, the power of hell will lose its grip over the soul of men. Those that are dead, their souls being free from the grip of hell shall be quickened by the presence of conscious immortal son of man to continue in paradise where Adam stopped. The dead I mean are those perfect souls in hell, those that have attained righteousness in their souls. When I said where Adam stopped I mean that they have to wait in paradise until when the son of man shall come again and their bodies that are in the dust shall attain a conscious immortality and enable their soul to live again eternal in a body. The entrance of an incorruptible flesh to hell was a great damage to Satan and hell because both of them lost their grip on righteous souls. Paul admonished the church saying:

> *And if Christ be in you, the body is dead because of sin, but the spirit is life because of righteousness. But if the spirit of him that raised up Jesus from the dead dwell in you, he that raised up Christ from the dead shall also quicken your mortal bodies by his spirit that dwelleth in you* (Rom. 8:10-11).

In the above Bible text, we have two spiritual empowerment mentioned by Paul, the first one is the spirit of Christ that restores us to the original spirit of paradise that Adam was created with and the second is the very breath and soul of the creator that is able to bring your mortal body to the conscious immortality, he referred to the former as Christ in you and the later as the Spirit of Him that raised up Christ from death.

God knew beforehand that it is impossible that man shall attain immortality in his fallen nature therefore in this agreement, he agreed to prepare in the womb of an innocent woman, an incorruptible body in order to descend with his very soul and breath into hell and set free the captivity of the captive. No man born from the beginning of the world have ever had incorruptible flesh except Jesus and there is no amount of sacrifices, offerings or prayers without Jesus that can help man to attain incorruptibility, all Man's righteousness was like filthy rag (Isa 64:6) and cannot save his soul from captivity, that was why Jacob God came in order to Jacob man into incorruptible.

> *Wherefore when he cometh into the world he saith, sacrifice and offering, thou wouldest not but a body has thou prepared me. In burnt offering and sacrifices for sin thou hast had no pleasure. Then said I, Lo, I come (in the volume of the book it is written of me) to do thy will O God* (Heb. 10:5-7).

The Jacob God from conception was formed incorruptible that was why Paul called him a quickening spirit, not a living soul like Adam. Having such incorruptible flesh does not give him advantage over pains and suffering because he felt in his flesh all that we feel in ours, the incorruptibility was only for him to effectively fulfill the God side of the Jacob God/Jacob man agreement. It follows that power of hell corrupts the flesh and holds in captive the soul which has no power on its own to exist without the body. If the body of the Messiah was corruptible, It would have remained in the dust and Satan

would not allow the soul to escape hell or the grip of hell would have held it. In another text about the Messiah, David prophesied saying:

> *For thou will not leave any soul in hell neither wilt*
> *thou suffer thy holy one to see corruption* (Ps. 16:10).

The above prophecy was of double reference it means, if the body of the Messiah would not see corruption and could be held by the grip of hell, it guaranted that the soul of David will be liberated in hell, not only David but all the righteous death and when he comes back (i.e. the Messiah) all the body of the righteous both the death and the living shall by his appearance attain conscious immortality or incorruptible and that is what we refer to as resurrection or rapture as it is referred to by many.

> *For the Lord himself shall descend from heaven*
> *with a shout, with the voice of the Archangel, and*
> *with the trump of God and the dead in Christ shall*
> *rise first. Then we which are alive and remain*
> *shall be caught up together with them in the*
> *clouds, to meet the Lord in the air and so shall*
> *we ever be with the Lord* (1 Thes 4:16-17).

Jesus was made an incorruptible flesh in order to ransom the corruptible Adamic flesh into incorruptible. His bodily resurrection could be question even as many do, because prophecy of his immortal body was earlier symbolized in the Tabernacle with shittem wood.

4:2 Oil – Christ; the anointed one.

The Spirit of the Lord GOD is upon me; because the LORD hath anointed me to preach good tidings unto the meek; he hath sent me to bind up the brokenhearted, to proclaim liberty to the captives, and the opening of the prison to them that are bound; To proclaim the acceptable year of the LORD, and the day of vengeance of our God; to comfort all that mourn (Isa. 61:1-2).

The ushering out of man at Eden was accompanied with bad news of suffering, sorrows, besiegement of the earth by the Satan, death, and imprisonment of soul in hell. From the day of Adam to the coming of Jesus man has been eking and out a living seeking a way to a fulfilled life, how to have solution to all these predicaments that befall him. Many generations went through war, some through cultism and other through all forms of human government that they might live a fulfilled life but to no avail. It takes only the mind of God who created man as to know the plans of God concerning the destiny of man and the way to attain to the fulfillment of life as it was originally ordained by God right from creation. Man has in every generation the knowledge that God shall one day liberate man from all these contradictions pose a great question for man. God already had a covenant with man for man's salvation. It needed a son of man who is Christ, fully anointed to know the mind of God as to fulfill the mind of God concerning man's redemption and salvation.

Looking at the above Isaiah text, it shows that the will of God embodied the Messiah with a lot of tasks for the liberation of man which task no man could accomplish unless he is Christ; the anointed one, he was also to be Christ in order to promulgate accurately the rules and ethics of the divine agreement with man and also fulfil them. It necessitated that the Messiah shall be Christ from heaven because man has through sin shot up the gate of heaven against himself, nobody therefore could be able to access heaven as to assist man. It needed therefore a supplanter of man that shall come down from heaven with the anointing necessary to accomplish this mission. Jesus says:

> *And no man hath ascended up to heaven, but he that came down from heaven, even the Son of man which is in heaven* (Jn. 3:13)

He was anointed as Christ in his first mission to inform men about the kingdom of God and its anointing that breaks all yokes, so that those that are languishing in the sorrows of suffering shall be comforted with new hope of liberation, to proclaim and demonstrate that man has authority through God's anointing to deliver himself and others from demonic operations and possessions. The anointing was also to enable him descend through death into hell and open the hell prison for the righteous souls, to inform men of his millennial reign on earth and also the day God will revenge the cause of men upon Satan. These were what Jesus accomplished from his era on earth and was revealed to mankind through the scriptures.

This Divine anointing upon the Messiah was the one that came down upon the Church at Pentecost and is working also through the generation of the church on earth. If we go through Isaiah 60 scripture from verse 3 he prophesied about the ministerial appointments of Jesus as fulfilled in Eph. 4:7-16. The Pentecost when the Holy Spirit gave beauty to the mortal men and the recognition given to the disciple at Antioch (Act 11:26). Verse 4 spoke about the conversion of the Gentiles that have lost the value of God for many generations. And verse 5 spoke about the feeding of the Apostles at Jerusalem by the Gentile church (2 Cor. 9). Verse 6 spoke about the first Christian council at Jerusalem that marks the beginning of church government or leadership. (Acts 15) Verse 7 was persecutions and the joy of the disciples for sharing in Christ suffering. The persecution also that helps to scatter them abroad and spread also the gospel. Verse 8 spoke about the Chastening and the leadership of the Holy Spirit in the Church affairs. Verse 9 emphasized on the universal church and universal Christians and their living standard different from the world standard. And verse 10 spoke about the joy of the perfected church that shall usher in the second advent of the Lord for the millennial reign (Eph. 4:12-16). Concerning the second anointing of the Messiah the Psalmist says:

> *Thy throne, o God is for ever and ever: the scepter*
> *of thy kingdom is a right scepter. Thou lovest*
> *righteousness, and hatest wickedness: therefore,*
> *God, thy God, hath anointed thee with the oil of*
> *gladness above thy fellows* (Isa. 45:6-7).

In the first advent of the Messiah, he was anointed as a messenger of God's covenant with man (Mal 3:1). But the anointing of the Second Advent is of a universal king Immortal and eternal. The oil of gladness not of sorrow like in his first advent where Isaiah 53 described him as a man of sorrows that was familiar with suffering. With this second anointing he will rapture the church, rule for 1000yrs and after the vengeance of our God, he shall rule as king forever. He has given us divine anointing through the Holy Spirit that we might attain perfection and rule in the millennium with him even forever. Jesus anointing was of divine sovereignty, to fill all creation with his spirit and have an everlasting sovereignty over creations. With divine scepter which cannot be taken away forever from him, he shall execute judgment and righteousness on earth. When he shall come. He shall arrive at Jerusalem with the raptured saints and restore the kingdom to Israel (Acts 1:6-7) and a Jerusalem city where the saints were to live and rule the earth with him for 1000 years (Rev. 20:4- 6).

In his millennial reign there shall live two types of men on earth, the immortal saints who shared in his anointing, who were privileged to meet with him in the cloud, they are to live in the beloved city of Jerusalem, while the rest of the mortal remains in their respective area upon the face of the earth. At his reign there shall be no death but he has the right scepter to put to death anyone who commits sin in that era. Death shall only be by execution not natural but the earth system shall continue as now, only there shall be no Satan for these 1000 years.

> *And I saw an angel come down from heaven, having the key of the bottomless pit and a great chain in his hand. And he laid hold on the dragon, that old serpent, which is the Devil, and Satan, and bound him a thousand years, and cast him into the bottomless pit, and shut him up, and set a seal upon him, that he should deceive the nations no more, till the thousand years should be fulfilled: and after that he must be loosed a little season.* (Rev. 20:1-3)

Like it is said before, the anointing that will usher in the Messiah in his second coming is not of sorrows and sufferings like the first was, this anointing like Isaiah 45:7 says, is with the oil of gladness. This anointing is also to usher in the Spirit of gladness that shall fill the whole earth and there shall be no more sorrow because the era of sorrow in the distance far away from God has gone. The Bible spoke about this era saying:

> *And it shall come to pass afterward that I will pour out my spirit upon all flesh; and your sons and daughters shall prophesy, your old men shall dream* dreams, **your young men shall see visions. And also upon the servants and upon the handmaids in those days will I pour out my spirit** (*Joel 2:28-29*).

This out pouring of Spirit is to all flesh upon the face of the earth, if we understand what "all" means, we should know that religion and race has no part to play here. This is Christ Millennial reign where he shares no authority with anyone but God, he is therefore in control of all flesh that walks upon the face of the earth without an upbraid he shall pour out his Spirit. restore kingdom for Israel (Joel 2:18-27). This anointing or poured out spirit shall sustain man alive for 1000 years (i.e. the mortal ones). When God created man, he never intended that man will serve him with his own strength. The moment he breathed into him, he wanted his spirit to work in man so that man will be able to say yes to his will at all-time but immediately man left Eden, the spirit of that anointing left him. It is the same spirit that the mortal man shall enjoy again in the millennium. Yet many shall like Adam rebel but the consequence is immediate execution and no resurrection for that person. The immortal saint, on the other hand that live with Christ in Jerusalem, shall never taste death again forever.

4:3 Incense –A Priest and advocate in prayer.

The LORD hath sworn, and will not repent; Thou art a Priest forever after the order of Melchizedek (Ps. 110:4).

Melchizedek was a Priest of God in Abraham's day. He was the king of Salem meaning king of peace and Salem was the Ancient name of Jerusalem. He met Abraham returning from his expeditious victory and with bread and wine in his hand, he blessed Abraham. Then Abraham gave him a tenth of the spoils he brought back from his expedition (Gen. 14:16-18). He was also called the king of righteousness. (Heb. 7:2).

He was also said to have no descent or genealogy. He had no recorded father, mother, birth or death. His genealogy was not recorded so that he could be a type of Messiah, who as God; has no beginning nor end and as man, his genealogy was not traced from the Aaronic Priesthood of Israel, yet he was to be a Priest forever (Heb. 7:3). The Priesthood of Melchizedek was older than Abraham who received God's promise of Jacob God/Jacob man redemption, with bread and wine he referred to the last supper of the Messiah. He who blessed Abraham was greater than Abraham according to the Scriptures and Abraham felt obligated to him and paid his tithe to him, showing the messiah to be Lord over Abraham. Jesus confirmed this episode in John's gospel that says thus:
Your father Abraham rejoiced to see my day: and he

> *saw it and was glad. Then said the Jews unto him.*
> *Thou art not yet fifty years old, and hast thou seen*
> *Abraham? Jesus said unto them. Verily, verily, I say*
> *unto you, before Abraham I am.* (Jn. 8:56-58).

I am that I am, the Ancient of days, he was God in the day of Abraham, when He established covenant with Abraham as Jacob God. Abraham saw his coming to pass through space and time in order to redeem humanity and stand a High Priest for them and offer a living and acceptable sacrifice once and for ever, and also to stand a gap between divinity and humanity. A High Priest in heaven reconciling humanity to God with one and eternal blood of his sacrifice. Concerning advents of the Messiah the Bible says:

> *Behold I will send my messenger, and he shall prepare*
> *a way before me: and the Lord, whom ye seek, shall*
> *suddenly come to his temple, even the messenger of the*
> *covenant, whom ye delight in: behold, he shall come,*
> *saith the LORD of hosts. But who may abide the day of*
> *his coming? And who shall stand when he appeareth?*
> *For he is like a refiner's fire, and like fuller's soap: and*
> *he shall sit as a refiner and purifier of silver: and he*
> *shall purify the sons of Levi and purge them as gold*
> *and silver, that they may offer unto the LORD an*
> *offering in righteousness. Then shall the offering of*
> *Judah and Jerusalem be pleasant unto the LORD, as in*
> *the days of old and as in former years (Mal 3:1-4).*

Whenever an earthly Aaronic High Priest is entering the temple of Jerusalem there were always messengers before him, shouting "Make way the High Priest is coming". John the Baptist did same to Jesus in the spirit of Elijah at the first coming and expecting Elijah to do same at his second coming as the Bible says:

> *Behold, I will send you Elijah the prophet before the*
> *coming of the great and dreadful day of the LORD: And*
> *he shall turn the heart of the fathers to the children,*
> *and the heart of the children to their fathers,*

lest I come and smite the earth with a curse (Mal. 4:5- 6).

John the Baptist worked in the spirit and power of Elijah, yet Elijah shall be coming to usher in the Divine High Priest at the second advent of Christ. In that era, the High Priest shall come with the raptured or first resurrected saints who shall be the Priests of our Lord in the millennium, replacing the mortal Aaronic Priests or the sons of Levi with the divine and redeemed saints, (Remember we have gold as a symbolic of divine and silver for redemption) It behooves the immortal saints to serve as priests before the Lord in that era because mortal man cannot stand before the majestic splendor, he shall come with them as to serve in the temple with him. It is only the redeemed saints that are capable of offering to the LORD an offering in righteousness.

The Messiah did not come in the generation of Aaronic priesthood but in the order of Melchizedek who blesses Abraham, who was to be the father of all nations. He came in this order so that he can make Priests of the redeemed from all nations and abolish the Aaronic priesthood which in Abraham it was something that never existed. He shall be the medium of worship for all creation, for at his name every knee shall bow and every tongue shall confess him as the Lord (Phil. 2:10-11). The incense in the Tabernacle was the symbol of worship, expressing that the Messiah was God to whom we offer worship from the beginning of humanity and that he shall come to offer eternal salvation with one sacrifice for mankind, the greatest worship ever known and become the medium of our worship to God. And as the Lord he shall be our High Priest forever.

4:4 Spices – Divine Love, the Love of God manifested.

Spices are substance used to give pleasant taste to food, but these ones here were used to give pleasant smell to incense and anointing oil signifying that with the Messiah, divine love shall be given to man through anointing and divine love shall be given or expressed to God through worship. Spices as English word means excitements or interests and the greatest excitements or interests is love. The Messiah therefore shall bring new and better excitements and interests through love, his spirit of love shall help man to love God with excitements and that spirit of love will bring new interest in worship. He demonstrated this mission with an allegory in the marriage of Canaan with wine and thus:

> *When the ruler of the feast had tested the water that was made wine, and knew not whence it was" (but the servants which drew the water knew ;) the governor of the feast called the bridegroom. And saith unto him, Every man at the beginning doth set forth good wine; and when men have well drunk, then that which is worse: but thou hast kept the good wine until now* (Jn. 2:9-10).

The Jews aristocrats at the first Advent of the Messiah, has God already well figured out in their human conceit, being drunk with the old and negative side of Jacob agreement that was in the law of Moses therefore they rejected the love of God which the Messiah came to impact in man. But the less privileged of the society embraced the love and was brought to the knowledge of God.

> *At that time Jesus answered and said, I thank thee, o*
>
> *Father, Lord of heaven and earth, because thou hast hid this thing from the wise and prudent, and hast revealed them unto babes. Even so, father for so it seemed good in thy sight* (Mtt. 11:25-26).

The Jews knew the anointing of God signified in oil, they also know the worship signified in incense but how to mix them with spices, they knew not therefore they went despising many sons and daughters of God they classified as sinners, especially the poor which they look upon as outcasts. It therefore needed the Jacob God to come and introduce the positive and everlasting side of the Jacob agreement that is embodied in love. For in love all the rules of the agreement are fulfilled. The law which were more of *"Thou shall not"*, were negative and creating in man negative attitude towards God and humanity. His coming therefore was to inform us of the love of God for man, how we can embrace this great love and how to convert it for the benefit of humanity. This law of love therefore creates a better and positive attitude in our service to God and humanity.

 The covenant God had with Abraham that was established in Jacob was not for Abraham but for the love that God has on the entire race of humanity. The discussions that emanated from this part of the covenant was thus as the Bible says:

> *Seeing that Abraham shall surely become a great and mighty nation, and all the nations of the earth shall be blessed in him?* (Gen. 18:18).
>
> *"And in thy seed shall all the nations of the earth be blessed; because thou hast obeyed my voice.* (Gen. 22:18).
>
> *And I will make thy seed to multiply as the stars of heaven, and will give unto thy seed all these countries; and in thy seed shall all the nations of the earth be*

blessed (Gen. 26:4).

The above texts confirmed that God's love and desire is to be a Jacob to the entire human race and He was to accomplish this through incarnating as the seed of Abraham. When God arrived as a Son therefore to fulfill this covenant, the Son; Jesus who was the Jacob God himself says:

> *For God so loved the world, that he gave his only begotten Son, that whosoever believeth in him should not perish, but have everlasting life. For God sent not his Son into the world to condemn the world; but that the world through him might be saved* (Jn. 3:16-17).

In order to fulfill His own side of the covenant of love God gave up His only begotten Son, to recompense the willingness of Abraham and his son Isaac according to the golden rule stipulated that says "the measure you mete shall be meted back to you", the rule of divine justice established in divine love. The Messiah, therefore, resolute in face of this covenant of love as he says:

> *Greater love hath no man than this, that a man lay down his life for his friends* (Jn. 15:13).

Even greater love he demonstrated in the agony of suffering and death he asked his father to forgive his enemies.

> *For they know not what they do (Lk 23:34).*

Jesus went through pains in trying to demonstrate the love of God to mankind, he emphasizes continuously in his messages that life has no meaning without love, owing to the fact that the spices of life is love. Concerning the greatest commandment, he says:

Jesus said unto him, Thou shalt love the Lord thy God with all thy heart, and with all thy soul, and with all thy mind.

> *This is the first and great commandment. And the second is like unto it, Thou shalt love thy neighbour as thyself. On these two commandments hang all the law and the prophets* (Matt. 22:37-40).

Loving God helps us to receive his love in order to offer spiritual worship acceptable to him and also to love our neighbour by giving ourselves to them. This is the only acceptable service in the sight of the Lord. I said in the beginning of this topic that the Spices here in the Tabernacle of God were used to give pleasant smell to incense and anointing oil, we know also that incense here represents priesthood and worship, and anointing oil represents anointing of the Lord. It follows, therefore, that without the love that the spices represent, there is neither effective priesthood, worship nor anointing, the implicit dimension of all these is to spice them with love else they become useless. Jesus emphasized on a more serious note how much humanity needed love to spice their relationship between man and God, and between man and man when he says:

> *But I say unto you, Love your enemies, bless them that curse you, do good to them that hate you, and pray for them which despitefully use you, and persecute you* (Matt. 5:44).

In another text he says:
Therefore, if thou bring thy gift to the altar, and there rememberest that thy brother hath ought against thee;
> *Leave there thy gift before the altar, and go thy way; first be reconciled to thy brother, and then come and offer thy gift* (Matt. 5:23-24)

Whatever Jesus Christ is, his anointing, his kingship, his priesthood, etc were spiced with love, without which they wouldn't have been effective. Paul was fully aware of this and knew that he himself cannot do less when he says:

> *Though I speak with the tongues of men and of angels, and have not charity, I am become as sounding brass, or a tinkling cymbal. And though I have the gift of prophecy, and understand all mysteries, and all knowledge; and though I have all faith, so that I could remove mountains, and have not charity, I am nothing. And though I bestow all my goods to feed the poor, and though I give my body to be burned, and have not charity, it profiteth me nothing* (1 Cor. 13:1- 3)

CHAPTER FIVE

Precious   Stones   and
Messiah.

5:1 Onyx Stones– Messiah of the Jews

G od commanded Moses to take two onyx stones and engrave the names of the children of Israel in the order of the twelve tribes on them, six names in one and six in the other respectively. He should make them to be set in ouches of gold and should put them upon the shoulders of the ephod as a memorial to the children of Israel. Aaron shall bear their names also before the Lord upon his two shoulders, for a memorial (Ex. 28:9-12).

These two onyx stones were to be made into brooches of gold base and be set on the shoulders of the sleeveless linen garment of Aaron, a garment covering only breast and back. Aaron was to wear this sleeveless garment always before the Lord. The ephod or sleeveless garment was made of gold, and of blue, purple, scarlet and fine twined linens. The symbol of the Messiah as God in gold, Prince and son of God in blue, king in purple, the Saviour in scarlet and the Perfect man in fine linen. The government of the Jews (Israel) shall he carry upon his shoulder as a memorial of God's everlasting covenant with the Jews and a sign of this covenant before God.

> *For unto us a child is born, unto us a son is given and*
> *the government shall be upon his shoulder and his name*
> *shall be called wonderful, counselor, the might God,*
> *the everlasting father, the prince of peace* (Isa. 6:9).

This scripture explains the ephod with the gold and of blue, purple, scarlet and fine linens. "Unto us" referred to Jewish people as a nation to who God's son will be born as the son of man and be given to be a sign of memorial to his covenant with Abraham established in Jacob. In another text he *says:*

> *Therefore, the Lord himself shall give you a sign.*
> *Behold a virgin shall conceive and bear a son, and shall call*
> *his name Emmanuel* (Isa. 7:14).

The Messiah shall be given as a memorial sign of God's redemptive covenant with Abraham for the world established in Jacob. When God finally gave a seed to Abraham by name Jacob He sealed the deal, changed Jacob's name to Israel and established the eternal covenant in Israel. In Israel therefore shall come the expected Messiah, the Supplanter, the Prince with God and man that is to prevail and have dominion over creation and that is why Paul referred to Jesus as the expected Messiah by saying.

> *For the Son of God, Jesus Christ, who was preached*
> *among you by us, even by me and Silvanus and*
> *Timotheus, was not yea and nay, but in him was yea.*
> *For all the promises of God in him are yea, and in him*
> *Amen, unto the glory of God by us* (1 Cor. 1:19-20).

Onyx which also means nail is cryptocrystalline quartz, veined and shelled, signifying that the Messiah shall be cryptic and shelled, his personality and meaning are to be concealed, he shall be a puzzle to the Jews, veined or so tender and lowering classed that they shall not recognize him as God among them. He shall be a crystal to the attitude and behaviour of the Jews, which will be offensive to them. Then shall they onyx (nail) him on the cross as a memorial between God and man in man's redemption. The first advent of the Messiah was for the Jews who were destined to offer him as a sacrificial lamb for the redemption of the whole world that is what Jesus emphasized to the Canaanite woman saying:

> *I am not sent but unto the lost sheep of*
> *the house of Israel* (Mtt. 5:24).

And to the Samaritan woman he says:

> *Ye worship ye know not what: we know what we*
> *worship: for salvation is of the Jews* (Jn. 4:22).

In another text we saw the Maggie saying:

> *Saying, where is he that is born King of the*
> *Jews? for we have seen his star in the east, and*
> *are come to worship him* (Matt. 2:2).

Another text speaks about the inscription upon the cross of Jesus saying:

> *And a superscription also was written over him*
> *in letters of Greek, and Latin, and Hebrew, THIS*
> *IS THE KING OF THE JEWS* (Lk. 23:38).

Aaron as the High Priest of Israel was to bear always before God, the ephod containing the names of the tribes of Israel upon his shoulders and by that he bears the burden and responsibility of all Israel before God. He alone made atonement for all their sins once a year, and if he should fail in his duty the whole Israel as a nation would perish. Isaiah foresaw the Messiah as a High Priest of the Jews, who is to shoulder the burden and responsibility of Israel before God, but he was puzzled by the onyx stone nature he shall appear with in his first advent to the Jews, he marveled and went on saying:

> *Who hath believed our report? And to whom is the arm*
> *of the Lord revealed for he shall grow up before him as a*
> *tender plant, and as a root out of a dry ground: he hath*
> *no form or comeliness and when we shall see him there is*
> *no beauty that we should desire him. He is despised and*
> *rejected of men a man of sorrows and acquainted with*
> *grief: and we hid as it were our faces from him; he was*
> *despised, and we esteemed him not. Surely he hath born*
> *our grieves and carried our sorrows: yet we did esteem*
> *him stricken, smitten of God, and afflicted. But he was*
> *wounded for our transgressions, he was bruised for*
> *our iniquities: the chastisement of our peace was upon*

him; and with his stripes we are healed (Isa. 53:1-5).

The cryptic and shelled nature of the Messiah made the report of his first advent hard for the Jews to believe, with tender and veiled personality he was seen by the Jews not good enough to be their Messiah, they rejected him and hid their faces from his crystal nature that reflect their evil behaviours towards God and humanity. In his suffering and at the cross the onyx stone was broken and its healing properties were made manifest. Onyx is a relatively hard stone with ranking of 7. 7 in Mohs ranking scale, the same as Quartz, commonly found in dust. Any gemstone with a ranking below 7 can easily be scratched, even by dust. Onyx is quite a tough stone due to its composition. but can crack or chip if dealt a hard blow. With reference to it therefore we could understand the stuff the Jewish Messiah was made of and how hard it is for him to crack or chip and why a hard blow was dealt on him during his passion. Concerning the Oynx stone Messiah Isaiah prophesied saying:

> *Therefore, thus saith the Lord God, Behold I lay in Zion for a foundation a stone, a tried stone, a precious corner stone, a sure foundation, he that believeth shall not make haste* (Isa. 28:16).
> *And he shall be for a sanctuary but for a stone of stumbling and for a rock of offence to both the houses of Israel for a gin and for a snare to the inhabitants of Jerusalem* (Isa. 8:14).

As we talk about the Messiah of the Jew, we are not to forget that the Oynx stone equally represents the Jews or the nation of Israel. If God did not make Israel an oynx stone the nation would have gone into extinction considering all they have gone through, from slavery, through war, besiegement, exile, dispersal, return and continuous war, yet they remain hard to break. Like the Onyx stone the cryptocrystalline quartz, veined and shelled, the Jewish nation is cryptic and shelled to be fully understood and also shelled by her enemies, yet she is a puzzle to the world and to her enemies. It was for peace to reign in a nation that is continuously at war, for whose sake he was onyxed or nailed to the cross, that his blood shall heal the nation and redeem it unto God. He shall be coming back to accomplish this peace mission in Israel. Jesus emphasized much that his first advent was limited to the Jews when he was sending out his disciples to preach he said to them:

> *Go not into the way of the Gentiles and into any city of the Samaritans, enter ye not. But go rather to the lost sheep of the house of Israel* (Mtt. 10:5-6).

He restricted them even not to interact with the Samaritans in this mission. The Samaritans as known were the Northerners in Israel. On the return of Israel from exile in Babylon, an alien population has dominated Samaria whom the king of Assyria deported to the Northern kingdom of Israel (1 Kg. 17:24) and the remnant of Israel in the Northern kingdom intermarried with them. During King Nehemiah's religious reformation in Judah, these people who the Jews had rejected and labeled Samaritans, went and built their own temple at Mount Gerizim. It was in 128 BC during the reign of the Jewish King Hyrcanus the temple was destroyed by the king on the ground that these people are no more Israelis. The people without temple still worshipped in the mountain the way Jews do at Jerusalem (Jn. 4:20). For Christ not to incorporate the Samaritans in this mission it means, it was strictly for the Jews. Paul the apostle who was very vast in the knowledge of the Oracles of God explained to the Roman how the covenant that was established in Jacob was first for the Jews as he says:

> *For I am not ashamed of the gospel of Christ: for is the power of God unto salvation to everyone that believeth, to the Jew first, and also to the Greek* (Rom. 1:16).
> *Tribulation and anguish, upon every soul of man that doeth evil, of the Jew first, and also of the Gentiles".* But *glory, honour, and peace, to every man that worketh good, to the Jew first, and also to the Gentile* (Rom. 2:9-10).

Salvation is for the Jews first and then the Gentiles because if Jesus had failed in his mission the whole nation of Israel would have perished. The salvation of the Jews is only to believe in Jesus as their Messiah.

5:2 OTHER PRECIOUS STONES – MESSIAH of all Nations

God commanded Moses to make a breastplate of judgment for Aaron, with the same materials used in the ephod, and with twelve different precious stones. The stones were: Sardius, topez, Carbuncle, Emerald, Ligure, Sapphire, Diamond, Agate, Amethyst, Onyx, Beryl and Jasper. They shall be set in gold enclosure. The names of the tribes of Israel shall be engraved on these precious stones respectively. And Aaron shall bear the names of the children of Israel in the breastplate upon his heart when he goeth into the holy place for a memorial before the Lord continually (Ex. 28:15-21, 29). The breastplate was made with the same material used in the ephod. It is also the symbol of the Messiah with the same personalities of the Messiah in the ephod. The Messiah shall bring in a gold enclosure or in a divine covenant both Jews and other nations or Gentiles and bear them in his heart before God. Bearing upon his heart the responsibilities of both Jews and Gentiles in life and death matters before the Lord God. As a High Priest he shall offer himself once and forever, with his blood he shall enter the Holy place of Heaven and atone once and forever the sins of the whole world. His blood shall be a continual and everlasting memorial of salvation for the entire world. This mission of saving the whole world shall not be done alone by the Messiah but with the other twelve precious stones with him, representing the Apostles. They shall share in his divine authority and inheritance in order to bring the gospel of salvation to the ends of the earth. The Messiah himself shall be their foundation and corner stone.

Jesus reaffirmed this in his post resurrection by informing his followers that it wasn't their business to be asking or to know when the Father will restore through him the kingdom to Israel. Their business he said, was to receive power, after the Holy

Spirit might have come upon them, so that they shall bear witness of salvation for him in Jerusalem, Judea, Samaria and to the ends of the earth (Acts 1:6-8). The onyx stone in the midst of other stones also signifies the presence of Jewish colony among other nations and also the Gentile proselytes among the Jews in the temple when this mission shall be fulfilled. It follows that since the Jewish exile in 6th century B.C, the Jews had begun to scatter around the whole of the Middle East and east of the Mediterranean.

As of the 1st century B.C they have made up a considerable population of many provinces under the then Greek empire. The deportation of Gentile population by Assyrians to Israel and the continuous reign of Gentiles over them have added a lot of Gentile proselytes to Jewish religion. The Jews at 1st Century B.C has in most of the main Greek cities a Jewish colony with its own synagogue (Acts 13:16,16:13). At this time the Old Testament (Septuagint) has been translated into Greek language and was used by the Hellenistic or Greek Jews (Acts 6:1) in their worships at those synagogues. Then at the fullness of time (Gal 4:4-5) when Jesus was born, the reign of Augustus of Rome has provided new roads that united the civilized world of that era, with its focus at Rome. With Latin and Greek as official languages, communication, therefore, became easier. Meanwhile the Hellenistic Jews provided readymade audience for the future Gospel preached by the Apostles and the Church of Jesus Christ. (Ps. 19:3-4).

> *And in that day there shall be a root of Jesse which shall stand ensign of the people, to it shall the Gentiles seek and his rest shall be glorious* (Isa. 11:10).

The Messiah shall stand as ensign or as a flag of the religious nation of Israel and in him shall other nations be religious and have rest in his glorious life. The breastplate that contained the precious stones was called the breastplate of judgment (Ex 28:15) and Paul in his letter to Ephesians mentioned breastplate of righteousness (Eph 6:14). Why was it called breastplate of

judgement? To answer this question Isaiah has this to say:
> *for when thy judgments are in the earth, the inhabitants*
> *of the world will learn righteousness* (Isa.
> 26:9).

In this Isaiah text, we can deduct also why Paul's Ephesians letter told the Gentile church that the breastplate is of righteousness. The coming of the Messiah was and is to establish judgments and righteousness and bring salvation to the ends of the earth.

> *Behold my servant, whom I uphold; mine elect, in whom*
> *my soul delighteth; I have put my spirit upon him he*
> *shall bring forth judgment to the Gentiles* (Isa. 42:1).

The Gentiles are placed in the breastplate of judgment signifying that the Messiah shall bring forth judgment to them. To establish to them the rules of righteousness, of sin and of judgement and this is the mission the Holy Spirit will accomplish with the Apostles and the Church of Jesus Christ so that the Gentiles shall be redeemed together with the Jews. Jesus related this information when he says:

> *Nevertheless, I tell you the truth; It is expedient*
> *for you that I go away: for if I go not away, the*
> *Comforter will not come unto you; but if I depart, I*
> *will send him unto you. And when he is come, he will*
> *reprove the world of sin, and of righteousness, and of*
> *judgment: Of sin, because they believe not on me;*
> *Of righteousness, because I go to my Father, and ye see me*
> *no more; Of judgment, because the prince of this world is*
> *judged* (Jn. 16:7-11).

Concerning the breastplate, the other precious stones and the Messiah, Isaiah continued to prophesy saying:

> *And now, saith the Lord that formed me from the*
> *womb to be his servant, to bring Jacob again to him,*
> *though Israel be not gathered, yet shall I be glorious in*
> *the eyes of the Lord, and my God shall be my strength.*
> *And he said, it is a light thing that thou shouldest*
> *be my servant to raise up the tribes of Jacob, and to*

> *restore the preserved of Israel: I will also give thee*
> *for a light to the Gentiles, that thou mayest be my*
> *salvation unto the end of the earth* (Isa. 49:5-6).

The Messiah was destined as Messiah for the entire world to be Jacob and Israel to men and bring them from every nation to be Jacobs and Israels to the glory of God. That he gathered not the entire lost sheep of the House of Israel shall not stop the glorious sacrifice on the cross, because all that he did was by the strength and will of the Father who established the boundaries and extent to which he was to conquer.

The Messiah was to raise up the tribes of Jacob which Jesus did by appointing his twelve Apostles according to the 12 tribes of Israel. These Apostles shall he preserve in Israel as pillars of his church to bring him as light to the Gentiles through Holy Spirit, so that salvation shall reach the ends of the earth. These are what other precious stones symbolized in the High Priest breastplate in the Oracles of God. The Gentiles are saved by their faith in the Messiah and by taking on the whole amour of God as written in Ephesians 6:13-18.

PART 2

In building the Tabernacle, we shall come to the knowledge of the missions of the Messiah from the Physical – Spiritual – Divine and eternal.

CHAPTER ONE

The Physical Mission of the Messiah Isa 61:1-2

1:1 THE FENCE OR THE OUTSIDE ENCLOSURE - THE

perfect wall. Symbolic of a Perfect man

For the enclosure, God commanded Moses, to make the enclosure out of fine (White) linen curtains, its South and North sides shall be 44 meters each, with twenty bronze base support posts and rod made of silver, the west side curtain should be 22 meters long, with ten posts and ten bases. All the equipment that is used in the tent and all the pegs for the enclosure are to be made of bronze (Ex. 27:9-15,19). A cord of Badger skins were tied at the silver hooks on top of the posts stretched to the bronze nails and be nailed alf way to the ground.

In this enclosure, we have the Messiah as the Tabernacle of the Lord's presence covered with fine (white) linen garment of perfect man; he was made perfect from conception by the power of the Holy Spirit, born of a virgin, without inherited sin or Adamic nature. He lived all his life perfectly that even his accusers had nothing to hold him with. He died an innocent death on trump-up charges, being guiltless and guileless he was made worthy in perfectness to bring many sons and daughters of Adam unto perfection. All religion and race of the earth know the exterior wall of Jesus as a perfect man, even Tom fool will not argue with you on the issue of Jesus being a perfect man.

Bronze or brass according to these oracles is a symbol of suffering The posts that held the wall being supported with bronze base signified the Messiah's perfect life was to make the creation perfect again, and he cannot achieve that unless he inherits in fullness the curse of Man's disobedience and be born a man of sorrow that is familiar with suffering. He shall stand upon suffering with his incorruptible flesh (the posts are made of shittim wood) to emerge triumphantly as a pillar of man's salvation. Silver as a symbol of redemption shows in the silver hooks that it is for our redemption that he was hooked up in cord (made of Badger skin) of trump up charges and rejection, nailed in suffering to death and was buried but he was to resurrect - that was why the bronze pegs were nailed half way to the ground to signify his death and resurrection.

The rod of silver signified (as the fine linen enclosure hang upon it) that it is for our redemption the perfect man was hung upon the tree. The thirty posts that supported the enclosure represents the years for him to enter into the public ministry.

In the final analysis, we found in the enclosure of this Tabernacle that the Messiah shall manifest to all men a perfect man from conception to death. In thirty years, this perfect man will be seen in public displaying the perfect God. His incorruptible flesh standing upon suffering will therefore pass through suffering and stand as a pillar of salvation. He shall suffer rejection and shall be hooked up in trump up charges for our redemption. He shall suffer and hang on the post to death, buried and resurrected. God also commanded Moses to make for an entrance to the Tabernacle a gate with curtains of 9 metres long made of fine (white) linen, woven with blue, purple and scarlet and decorated with embroidery, it is to be supported by four posts and four bases of bronze (Ex. 27:16).

No man cometh unto the father but by him, Jesus is the way, He is the Messiah, with a very high interwoven personality that needed a careful and close inspection of a knowledgeable man in other to figure out these personalities. In fine linen he was a perfect man, in blue he was a son of God or prince, in scarlet a Saviour and in purple a king and interwovenly he was the Messiah. The gate of the Tabernacle was made at the east side of the enclosure like the gate of Eden signifying the Messiah as the way back to Eden.

> *So he drove out the man; and he placed at the east of the garden of Eden Cherubims and a flaming sword which turned everyway, to keep the way to the tree of life* (Gen 3:24).

The gate of the Tabernacle is the way to the tree of life. Therefore:

> *Enter ye in at the straight gate, for wide is the gate and broad is the way that leadeth to destruction, and many there be which go in there at. Because straight is the gate and narrow is the way which leadeth unto life and few there be that find it* (Mtt. 7:13-14).

When man was chased out of paradise or Eden, the angels of God kept guard with flaming sword against man. The terror seen by man in the east gate of Eden made man to go astray, in a distance far away from Eden he languished in suffering unto death. Man's ultimate desire is a way back to paradise and in Messiah God has descended to be our way, he is now the East Gate of paradise for all that want to come to God through him.

1:2 The Alter of Sacrifice. - The sacrificial lamb

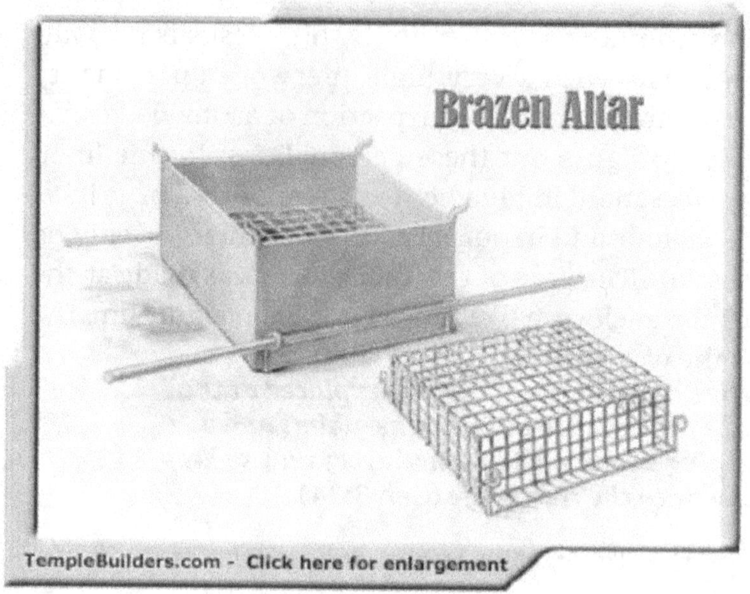

For the altar of sacrifice, God commanded Moses to make an altar out of Shittim wood, it was to be, square 2.2 meters long and 2.2 meters wide, 1.3 meters high. To make projections at the top of the four corners, they are to form one piece with the altar and the whole is to be covered with bronze, make shovels, bowls, hooks and fire pans, all the equipment should be made of bronze. To also make the altar out of boards and leave it hollow according to the plan he was shown on the mountain by God (Ex. 27:1-4, 8. 38:1-7). In the altar of sacrifice, we see the Messiah in shittim wood as an incorruptible flesh from conception to death, the Jacob God who shall ransom for the sin of the world, his sacrifice shall project to the four ends of the earth to gather the whole world in one piece with the Jews to God the father. The Jewish Nation becomes the altar of sacrifice in which the Messiah should be sacrificed for the whole world to be saved in one piece with the Jews.

The altar being overlaid or covered with bronze was to be sign of suffering of the Messiah on the altar of sacrifice. The altar of sacrifice itself signifying the Jewish nation, which denotes that in Israel shall Messiah suffer overlaid from conception to death as a sacrifice for Jewish salvation and a sacrifice projected to annex the four ends of the earth. His incorruptible flesh shall be overlaid in the immensity of suffering unto death, but he shall be hollowed that is to say without sin, guiltless and guileless and able to triumph over death and hell. The whole altar and its projections were covered with bronze to express that both Jews and the four ends of the earth shall have share in his suffering. In his suffering it shall involve both Jews and Gentiles, the Jews shall as the altar of sacrifice project him to the Gentile in his suffering and death. The same way shall the Gentile share with him in suffering and with the Jews in the salvation that shall come out of the suffering. The bronze shovels in the equipment shows that this suffering of the Messiah shall bring him down to the grave and as shovels are used in the Tabernacle to add coal to the fire in the brazen altar it then signifies that through the grave he shall descend into hell before he shall accomplish this sacrifice. As the bowels are used in collection of blood of animals sacrificed, it shows that there shall be a blood shed in this sacrifice of suffering and death, and it is that blood that shall be collected for the atonement of the world sin and in hooks we saw the symbols of him being hanged in suffering and like through a fire pan shall he suffer for the redemption of humanity. In these hooks of suffering and death shall he hook up the divine court to cancel the death sentence on man and also hook God up with man in reconciliation and all nations together for God.

In the final analysis, the Messiah, the Jacob God, was to Jacob humanity as an incorruptible man, to be surrounded with suffering from conception to death as the Bronze utensils surrounded the brazen altar. On the cross, he was to be covered with suffering in his incorruptible flesh as through a brazen fire pan, died and buried, though he was hollow without sin, in the hollow through his body he shall pour out his blood for the sin of Israel and the whole world. Israel herself was to be the altar of sacrifice where the Messiah was to be the sacrificial lamb. Through this sacrifice salvation shall project from the altar to the four ends of the earth so that the whole world with Israel shall be one piece serving one God. With this sacrifice shall humanity be back to paradise.

> *Behold, I have refined thee, but not with silver, I have chosen thee in the furnace of affliction for mine own sake, will I do it: for how should my name be polluted? And I will not give my glory unto another* (Isa. 48:10- 11). *The Messiah was not refined with silver, which means that he was not redeemed, (silver is the symbol of redemption) but in brazen furnace of affliction he redeemed others.*

1:3 The Laver- Sanctification, renewal, refreshing, Glorious existence through suffering

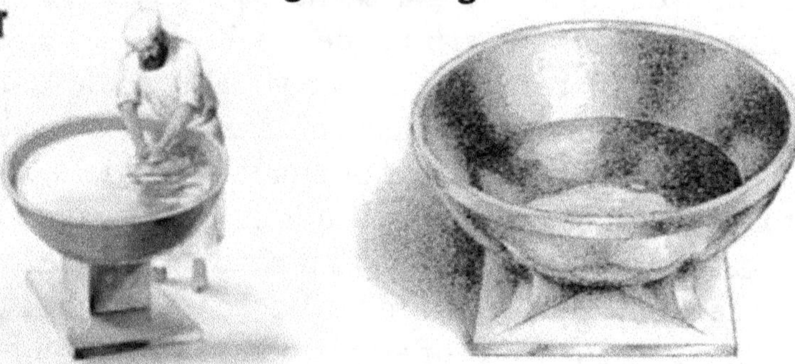

The Lord God commanded Moses to make a bronze basin with a bronze base, place it between the altar and the tent and put water in it. Aaron and his sons are to use the water to wash their hands and feet before they go into the tent or approach the altar to offer food offering. Then they will not be killed. (Ex 30:17-21). The bronze basin was made of bronze Mirrors collected from women. The basin being made of bronze signifies suffering and humiliation but in its shining mirror surface signified glory, divine glory. It then means that his suffering and humiliation was to be his immediate step to exaltation and glory. As he suffers unto death he shall shine in resurrection to bring to glory the immensity of God's love for humanity. He was to the reflection of God's glory to humanity and a perfect image of God on earth: that he shall bring the knowledge of God to humanity. Jesus at the end of his mission on earth said:

I have glorified thee on the earth. I have finished the work which thou givest me to do. And now, o father, glorify thou me with thine own self with the glory which I had with thee before the world was (Jn. 17:4-5).

He was to suffer to the glory of God on earth to establish God's righteous judgment upon the earth. Confirming God's ability to do all it takes to see that justice is done and humanity also is saved. By his suffering and death, he reflected unto man the faithfulness and righteousness of God which no circumstance can hinder, thereby, pointing out in reflection that God is of righteousness who can never go back on his promises. In the mirror surface it signifies that standing before the Messiah is to mirror your image and attitude in the glorious light of God. Coming in contact with him means to measure your behaviour in the presence of the glory of God. In him is nothing about man hidden, to him is nothing hidden and for him shall nothing be hidden. To whoever that comes to him shall the mystery of God be revealed to, for in him is nothing hidden about God. He is the light of the glorious image of God presented in more clearly perceptive to humanity.

The water in the basin signifies renewal, regeneration, resurrection and refreshing. The water also is symbolic of words of God as it filled the basin and the basin becomes its container so shall the Messiah be a human body that contained the word of God, for renewal, regeneration, resurrection and refreshing.

Sacrifice and offering thou didst not desire; my ears has thou opened: burnt offering and sin offering hast thou not required. Then said I Lo, I come: in the

> *volume of the book it is written of me I delight to do thy
> will, o my God: yea, thy law is within my heart I have
> preached righteousness in the great congregation lo,
> I have not refrained my lips, o Lord, thou knowest. I
> have not hid thy righteousness, within my heart; I have
> declared thy faithfulness and thy loving kindness and
> thy truth from the great congregation (Ps. 40:6-10).*

This prophecy concerning the Messiah signifies in the Laver that God is no more interested in sustaining the life of Israel with continuous sacrifices. The Messiah should abolish the sacrifice with his own self at the brazen altar and annex to the laver or the Bronze basin where the law of righteousness that gives access to the throne of God is established. The law of the spirit by which we have access to God and without which we are dead. The Messiah as the Laver filled with water, has divinely opened ear to have no stop of ear to God and His word, he is the word of God himself "in the volume of the book", reflecting the will of God to humanity by preaching God's righteousness to man. Standing before the great congregation as God's image and reflection of the mysteries of God. In him was nothing hidden and upon the cross he declared even more to the great congregation the faithfulness of God in promises, loving kindness to humanity, and the truth of divine intervention to save humanity. By the word of God there is always the renewal of heart and access to God.

> *That he might sanctify and cleanse it with the
> washing of water by the word (Eph. 5:26).*

The physical mission of the Messiah as depicted in the Oracles of God were to bring to mankind the perfect way of life and what it takes to be perfect as we saw in the perfect enclosure of fine (White) line that fenced the Tabernacle. In his teaching Jesus confirmed this as he says:

> *But I say unto you, love your enemies, bless them that
> curse you, do good to them that hate you, and pray for
> them which despitefully use you, and persecute you;*

> *That ye may be the children of your Father which is in*
> *heaven: for he maketh his sun to rise on the evil and*
> *on the good, and sendeth rain on the just and on the*
> *unjust. Be ye therefore perfect, even as your Father*
> *which is in heaven is perfect (Matt. 5:44-45, 48).*

He is to reveal to humanity the personality we lost when Adam fall. In his personality, we saw an interwoven qualities as follows: in fine (white) linen he was a perfect man, in blue he was a son of God or prince, in scarlet a Saviour and in purple a king and interwovenly he was the Messiah, this is the divine nature he brought for us to share with him. Apostle Paul spoke of this when he says:

> *The first man is of the earth, earthy: the second man*
> *is the Lord from heaven. As is the earthy, such are*
> *they also that are earthy: and as is the heavenly,*
> *such are they also that are heavenly. And as we have*
> *borne the image of the earthy, we shall also bear*
> *the image of the heavenly (1 Cor. 15:47-49).*

As a sacrificial lamb, a lamb led to slaughter, the lamb that was slain, we saw the Messiah in the brazen altar made of shittim wood overlaid with brass, an incorruptible flesh from conception enshrouded (overlaid) in suffering and was a sacrifice for atonement, the Jacob God who shall ransom for the sin of the world. At the four ends of the altar were four projected horns that depict how the sacrifice shall project to the four ends of the earth to gather the whole world in one piece with the Jews to God. The altar itself where the four horns were attached represent also the Jewish Nation where the Messiah shall be sacrificed for the whole world to be saved in one piece with the Jews. Concerning this, the Bible says:

> *The next day John seeth Jesus coming unto*
> *him, and saith, Behold the Lamb of God, which*
> *taketh away the sin of the world (Jn. 1:29).*

As he is our suffering and sacrificial Messiah, in the bronze laver he represents our sanctification, renewal, **regeneration,** refreshing, righteousness, and our glorious existence through his suffering and death. Like the shining surface of the Laver, the Messiah reflects the glory of God, he manifests the glory of God to us, we mirror ourselves in him, we hide our face from him as he reflects our wickedness. His words are like the water that fills the Laver, he is the water of life, for our righteousness, our refreshing, regeneration and sanctification without which we are not worthy to enter the kingdom nor the presence of God. He is the word of God and the water into which we are baptized, without which we cannot be members of the household of God.

> *Jesus answered, Verily, verily, I say unto thee, except a man be born of water and of the Spirit, he cannot enter into the kingdom of God* (John 3:5).

It takes his sacrifice at the brazen altar for him to make the Laver available for us, in his post resurrection appearance, he confirmed the availability of the Laver and assured his disciples that he has dealt and finished all the altar of sacrifice required. The duties therefore, starts from the Laver. That is why the Bible says:

> *And he said unto them, Go ye into all the world, and preach the gospel to every creature. He that believeth and is baptized shall be saved; but he that believeth not shall be damned. And these signs shall follow them that believe; In my name shall they cast out devils; they shall speak with new tongues* (Mk. 16:15- 17).

.

CHAPTER TWO

The Spiritual Mission of the Messiah.

2:1   The Outer Veil - The outer veil-entrance to Holy tent (Isa. 61:3-6)

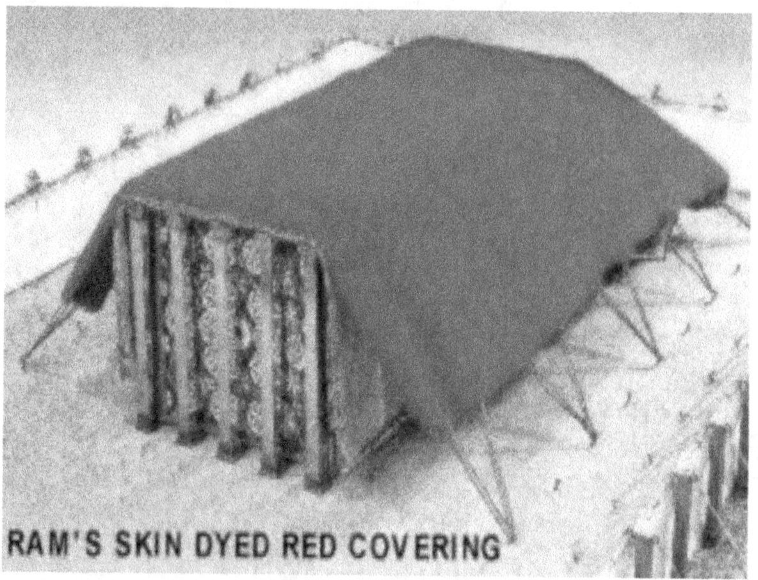

God commanded Moses to make an entrance to the Holy tent with a curtain of fine linen woven with blue, purple and scarlet and he decorates it with embroiling. Five posts of shittim wood covered with gold with five bronze bases as their standing bases and the posts to be fitted gold hooks (Ex. 26:36-37). This is symbolic of the Messiah interwoven personality of a perfect man, prince of God and man, king and Saviour in the glory of the Almighty and being made beautiful like an embroidery in the interwoven curtains that represent his personality. At this stage he is a Spiritual guide to our destiny and a spiritual Lord over humanity, he has become a spiritual guide for the perfection of humanity, reconciling with God many sons and daughters spiritually, giving them spiritual authorities to be kings as to help in bringing others unto salvation.

The five shittim wood post overlayed with gold are symbolic of the Messiah's spiritual five arms of ministries that were in him and were later given to mankind, in him is found an Apostle sent by God Himself, an evangelist as he went about preaching, a pastor as he coordinates the affairs of men and a teacher as he was fondly called. These were full ministry of God embodied in him and these were equally the offices he shared to mankind, as the Bible says:

> *And he gave some <u>apostles,</u> and some and some <u>prophets</u> and some <u>evangelists</u> and some <u>pastors</u> and <u>teachers</u>. For the perfecting of the saints, for the work of ministry, for the edifying of the body of Christ. Till we all come in the unity of the faith, and of the knowledge of the son of God unto a perfect man, unto the measure of the stature of the fullness of Christ. That we henceforth be no more children tossed to and fro and carried about with every wind of doctrine, by the sleight of men, and cunning craftiness, whereby they lie in wait to deceive. But speaking the truth in love, may grow up unto him in all things which is the head, even Christ. From whom the <u>whole body fitly joined together</u> and compacted by that which every joint supplieth, according to the effectual working in the measure of every part, maketh increase of the body unto the edifying of itself in love* (Eph. 4:11-16).

The gold hooks fitted on the posts that also fitted the curtain on the posts signify the spiritual ministries of Christ that is inseparable but rather work together as one because they are of one body which is Christ. These ministries he gave to his body the church to work with as one inseparable Church on earth. These ministries in the church are fitly joined together as Christ is not divided but one individual as the whole ministries worked together in him, so he expected that the church remain one and the ministries should work together for the edification of the Church.

> *Then said Jesus unto them again, Verily, verily, I say unto you, I am the door of the sheep. All that ever came before me are thieves and robbers: but the sheep did not hear them. I am the door: by me if any man enter in, he shall be saved, and shall go in and out, and find pasture* (Jn 10:7-9).

This entrance is the real entrance to the sheepfold. The

outside gate can receive and any Tom, Dick and Harry but not this door, this door is the main entrance into the body of Christ. Before and after the coming of the Messiah many have posed as perfect men and many more pretended to be the entrance gate to the Tabernacle. Many have even faked the qualities of Christ personality at the gate. They led their followers to nowhere, even to their premature death. This door to the Holy tent is different, not only that it is supported by four posts but were embroidered to be more beautiful and glorious, the extra quality only the begotten Son of God could have.

> *And the Word was made flesh, and dwelt among us, (and we beheld his glory, the glory as of the only begotten of the Father,) full of grace and truth* (John 1:14).

This territory is not for novice but for those sanctified at the laver and they are nothing short of the priests of the Most High God. Only them that are worthy to approach the door to the sheepfold. When Jesus says:

> *I have given them thy word; and the world hath hated them, because they are not of the world, even as I am not of the world. Sanctify them through thy truth: thy word is truth* (Jn 17:14, 17).

Jesus has actually brought his disciples to the Laver when he made this statement so that they will receive the baptism at his death and resurrection. His death did not only complete their baptism he ushered them through the door into the closed door of the Holy Tent where the Church was born at Pentecost. Jesus washed his disciples clean with his word, I said earlier that the water in the Laver represents the word of God and that was what Jesus has given them enough and in his post resurrection he appeared to them and opened their understanding to the words so that they shall be sanctified for the Spiritual rebirth. He told his apostles saying:

> *Now ye are clean through the word which I have spoken unto you* (Jn. 15:3).

Paul also clearly informed the Ephesians that water

represents the word as he says:

That he might sanctify and cleanse it with the washing of water by the word (Eph. 5:26).

2:2 The Interior - The interior of the Holy tent

God commanded Moses to make the interior of the sacred tent, the tent of the Lord's presence out of ten pieces of fine linen woven with blue, purple and scarlet, and embroided with figures of winged creatures, to sew five of them in one set and do the same with the other five. To make loops of blue cloth on the edge of the outside pieces in each set, make fifty gold hooks with which to join the two set into on piece (Ex. 26:1, 3-4,6). This is the symbol of the Kingdom of God ushered in at the Pentecost to form the Church. This interior represents Christ and the body of Christ. The coming of the Holy Spirit brought in the reign of Christ upon those that believed and being under this reign therefore they became members of the kingdom of God and the members of the Church of Christ, that is what is represented in this interior. In this Spiritual mission of the Messiah we should understand the Holy Spirit as Jesus Christ Unlimited, because that is what these Oracles expressed here. Jesus also confirmed it in these

Bible texts as he says:

> *I will not leave you comfortless: I will come to you.*
> *Yet a little while, and the world seeth me no more;*
> *but ye see me: because I live, ye shall live also. At*
> *that day ye shall know that I am in my Father,*
> *and ye in me, and I in you* (Jn. 14:18-20).
> *Verily I say unto you, there be some standing here, which*
> *shall not taste of death, till they see the Son of man*
> *coming in his kingdom* (Matt. 16:28).
> *And he said unto them, Verily I say unto you, that there*
> *be some of them that stand here, which shall not taste of*
> *death, till they have seen the kingdom of God come with*
> *power* (Mk. 9:1).
> *But I tell you of a truth, there be some standing here,*
> *which shall not taste of death, till they see the kingdom*
> *of God* (Lk. 9:27).

Jesus informed his disciple that he would come and comfort them but not physically anymore, no physical eyes can see him anymore but them that he was going to live spiritually in them and with them. He further informed them that he was coming soon as many of them are still alive to establish his kingdom. If he was not the comforter that returned, ushering in the Kingdom of God at Pentecost, then who did? It is the same Jesus who came for his spiritual mission as expressed in the Oracles. Beyond the door which is Christ and his five arm ministry is the tent of the Lords present. Paul described the atmosphere of this place when he says:

> *But ye are come unto mount Sion, and unto the city*
> *of the living God, the heavenly Jerusalem, and to an*
> *innumerable company of angels, To the general assembly*
> *and church of the firstborn, which are written in heaven,*
> *and to God the Judge of all, and to the spirits of just*
> *men made perfect, And to Jesus the mediator of the new*
> *covenant, and to the blood of sprinkling, that speaketh*
> *better things than that of Abel* (Heb. 12:22-24).

Let's now understand the tent, the interior of the sacred tent, the tent of the Lord's presence was made out of the qualities of the Messiah's personality. They are ten pieces of fine linen woven with blue, purple and scarlet, the interwoven linens that represent the Perfect man, the Son of God, the King, and the Saviour and the embroidery figures of winged creatures, represent the innumerable company of angels. The linens were made into ten piece, five of these linens were sewn in one set and the same went with the other five to represent the five arms of the ministry of the angels and men joined together to form the Church of Christ. The loops of blue on the edge of the outside pieces in each set, was blue cloths in u shape crossing each other to form the sign of the cross on which the Son of God was crucified. The fifty gold hooks with which to join the two sets of the curtain together expressed that he returned in fifty days in the company of the Angels to join the two churches in one piece. The fifty days marked the Pentecost, the day when Jesus baptized his followers with the Holy Ghost and fire.

> *And when the day of Pentecost was fully come, they were all with one accord in one place. And suddenly there came a sound from heaven as of a rushing mighty wind, and it filled all the house where they were sitting. And there appeared unto them cloven tongues like as of fire, and it sat upon each of them. And they were all filled with the Holy Ghost, and began to speak with other tongues, as the Spirit gave them utterance* (Acts 2:1-4).

The Messiah arrived at Pentecost riding upon the wing of the wind in the company of his angels that form the mighty wind. The Bible says:

> *He bowed the heavens also, and came down; and darkness was under his feet. And he rode upon a cherub, and did fly: and he was seen upon the wings of the wind* (2 Sam. 22:10-11).

In addition to what Samuel saw the Psalmist described the Pentecost day he saw when he says:

> *Who layeth the beams of his chambers in the waters: who maketh the clouds his chariot: who walketh upon the wings of the wind. Who maketh his angels*

spirits; his ministers a flaming fire (Ps. 104:4).

We now conclude with the above texts that the Messiah returned for his spiritual mission, riding upon the Cherub in the wings of the wind. In this mission his Church assumed his body having his full qualities of his interwoven personality as the Perfect man, Son of God, King and Saviour, whatever he was when he was on earth the Church now becomes and even more because the church lives in his holy presence. The interior of this tent represents both the spiritual presence of Christ and the body of Christ the church in his spiritual presence, whenever the church gathered, it is the gathering of spirits because both the angels and men born of the Spirit that form the church are all spirits.

> ***That which is born of the flesh is flesh; and that***
> ***which is born of the Spirit is spirit*** (Jn. 3:6).

This Tent of the Lord's presence proves that the church is Spiritual and the members of the Church of Christ are spirits, no man can be part of this spiritual tent unless he is born of the water of the Laver and the Spirit of Pentecost the established the tent (the church). The analysis of this tent also disproved the idea that the church is the bride of Christ. The church is called the body of Christ, and a perfect man (Eph 4:12-13). The church therefore is a man and cannot be a bride. Christians or the church is called the children of the bride chamber (Mtt 9:15) the children of the bride chamber cannot be the bride. The bride should be the holy Jerusalem where the church will dwell (Rev. 21:9-10). The embroidery winged creatures in the curtains signifies the presence of God's angels in the church, who also will help in bringing the church unto salvation. Of the angels Paul says:

> ***Are they not all ministering spirits, sent***
> ***forth to minister for them who shall be***
> ***heirs of salvation*** (Heb. 1:14).

At Pentecost (Acts 2:1-13) God gathered the church in one piece, the children of men he gathered at Jerusalem from diverse places, at the feast of Pentecost. Then he gathered the angels with the rushing sound of mighty wind to join the church together with the divine hooks of the Holy Spirit which is Jesus Christ unlimited. When Psalm 104:4 referred to Pentecost and the coming of the Holy Spirit it says "The beam of his chambers in the waters" referring to Genesis 1:2 and the Psalmist confirmed that the coming of the Holy Spirit on Pentecost shall be in the wings of the wind, bringing the angels together as spirits, and ministers he made a flaming fire. This "flaming fire" seen in the tongues of fire upon the whole ministers at Pentecost representing one Spirit of the Messiah.

In this topic, the whole emphasis is that the crucified physical Messiah shall return as spiritual Messiah, fill the church with his presence and the church will represent him on earth as his body. Bringing together in one piece to form the church two sets of ministers of the Messiah, one set as Angels and the other as men, in fifty days that marked the Pentecost; marking also the beginning of the universal church, with cross as the sign of the church as a prince with God and man that have prevailed. Jesus earlier informed us that the gate of hell has no power over the church because he is the church and has conquered hell.

2:3 Golden Lamp Stand - Golden lampstand

God commanded Moses to make a lampstand of pure gold, make its base and its shaft of hammered gold, its decorative flowers including buds and petals, are to form one piece with it, six branches are to have three decorative flowers, shaped like almond blossoms with buds and petals. The shaft with four decorative flowers. And one bud is to be below each of the three pairs of branches. The buds, the branches and the lamp stand are to be a single piece of pure hammered gold. To make its tongs and trays of pure gold, using 35kg of pure gold to make them according to the plan that God showed him on the mountain (Ex. 25:31-40). The lampstand has six branches with one directly out of its shafts making the total of seven lamps in the stand. The lampstand was called candlestick. (Ex. 37:17) and it was kept at the South side of the Holy tent.

The lamp stand is symbolic of the eyes of the Lord upon his body, the church (Zech. 4:2, 10), the seven churches of first born written in heaven (Rev. 1:12-13,20;2:1, Heb. 12:23) and also the seven spirits of God, or the fullness of the Holy Spirit; the Messiah unlimited (Rev. 4:5, 5:6). It is the illumination, inspiration, revelation, and the divine knowledge of God's perfect will for the church. The divine inheritance of the church. The candlestick or the lampstand was made entirely of pure gold to signify that it represents something that is purely divine. The Holy Ghost in the church ushered in by the Messiah at Pentecost. The lampstand shafts are made of hammered gold, hammered as symbolic of Judgment.

> *And when he is come, he will reprove the world*
> *of sin, and of righteousness, and of judgment: of*
> *righteousness, because I go to the father, and ye*
> *see me no more, of judgment because the prince*
> *of this world is judged* (Jn 16:8, 10-11).

When the Holy Spirit; the Messiah unlimited will return, he will be a reprover and establisher of the rules of rights against all wickedness and against the satanic operation in the church. To give the church the authority and direction to right judgment, authority and dominion he came to establish. The lampstands having 3 pairs of lamps in each side like a scale to depict the scale of justice, the eyes of the Lord upon the church, running to and fro in the activities of the church that he might use the church to bring right and justice to the world. The lampstand also represents the seven spirit of God or the fullness of the Holy Spirit in the church and according to Isaiah the seven spirits of God are the spirits of righteousness which are the spirits of the Messiah, called the spirit of the Lord. It is represented in the first branch of the lamp that proceeded directly from the shaft. Others are spirit of wisdom, understanding, counsel, might, knowledge and the fear of the Lord. The sevenfold anointing of the Messiah given to the church, the fullness of the Holy Spirit. As we can see in the lamp, the main shaft is the Messiah and these seven spirits procced from him.

> *And the spirit of the LORD shall rest upon him,*
> *the spirit of wisdom and understanding, the spirit*
> *of counsel and might, the spirit of knowledge*
> *and of the fear of the LORD* (Isa. 11:2).

The seven candlesticks also represent the seven churches of the first born written in heaven. These seven churches are represented with the characteristics given in Revelation 2-3 with names as Ephesus, Smyrna, Bergamos, Thyatira, Sardis,

Philadelphia and Laodicea. They are the seven churches with seven spirits of God and seven guardian angels. As long as there is only one lampstand with seven branches in the tent built by Moses, it shows that all the Christ body on earth fall under this seven churches of the first born. Each individual with his individual character is spiritually fitted into these churches according to the characters of each and every one of them described by Jesus in Revelation. The decorative flowers of the lampstand represent the divine diadem of the church, the diversities of spiritual gifts given to the church as the flowers are three in each lamp stick, they depict the diversities of spiritual gifts grouped in three as revelations, inspirations and might and finally from Isaiah we read thus:

> *For Zion's sake will I not hold my peace, and for Jerusalem's sake I will not rest, until the righteousness thereof go forth as brightness, and the salvation thereof as lamp that burneth. And the Gentiles shall see thy righteousness and all kings thy glory: and thou shall be called by a new name, which the mouth of the LORD shall name. thou shalt also be a crown of glory in the hand of the LORD and a royal diadem in the hand of thy God* (Isa. 62:1-3).

Isaiah refers to the Messiah's spiritual mission in lampstand, lighting up the spiritual church at mount Zion and in heavenly Jerusalem and the church on earth spiritually *"until the righteousness thereof go forth as brightness, and the salvation thereof as lamp that burneth. And the Gentiles shall see thy righteousness and all kings thy glory"*. It is at this spiritual era that the Messiah becomes a light to the Gentiles as Isaiah rightly Prophesied saying:

> *And he said, it is a light thing that thou shouldest be my servant to raise up the tribes of Jacob, and to restore the preserved of Israel: I will also give thee for a light to the Gentiles, that thou mayest be my salvation unto the end of the earth* (Isa. 49:6).

Simeon confirmed this prophesy when Jesus was brought to

him by saying:

For mine eyes have seen thy salvation, which
thou hast prepared before the face of all
people; a light to lighten the Gentiles, and the
glory of thy people Israel (Lk. 2:30-32).

Somebody may ask, what is the prove that this mission to the Gentile shall be in his spiritual era or after his resurrection and Pentecost? The answer is that these Oracles of God say so and it is seconded by this text of the Bible that says:

That Christ should suffer, and that he should be the
first that should rise from the dead, and should shew
light unto the people, and to the Gentiles (Acts 26:23).

Another text confirmed that the Messiah will reach the Gentiles spiritually through his church, by saying:

But when the Jews saw the multitudes, they were
filled with envy, and spake against those things which
were spoken by Paul, contradicting and blaspheming.
Then Paul and Barnabas waxed bold, and said, It
was necessary that the word of God should first
have been spoken to you: but seeing ye put it from
you, and judge yourselves unworthy of everlasting
life, lo, we turn to the Gentiles. For so hath the Lord
commanded us, saying, I have set thee to be a light
of the Gentiles, that thou shouldest be for salvation
unto the ends of the earth (Acts 13:45-47).

The Messiah commanded the Church, his body which Paul and Barnabas represent, to work according to his spiritual mission, to be light to the Gentiles and be for salvation to the ends of the earth. Is the church now the light? No, the Messiah remains the light but having given his divine nature to the church, the church now become the lamp that brings the light to the Gentiles. The church here can be described as the man who share in the Divine nature of the Messiah, whose name is written in heaven, whose gathering is at mount Zion; the heavenly Jerusalem, who is commissioned to share with the Messiah in his spiritual mission. in affirmative a Hebrew text says:

But ye are come unto mount Zion, and unto the city of the living God, the heavenly Jerusalem, and to an innumerable company of angels. To the general assembly and the church of firstborn which are written in heaven and to God the Judge of all, and to the spirits of just men made perfect (Heb. 12:22-23).

2:4 TABLE OF SHEW BREAD

God commanded Moses to make a table of shittim wood length 4ft 2in, breadth 2ft 1in, height 3ft 1½in overlay it with pure gold. To make a gold crown round it and a border about 4in around the table. To make a golden crown to the border and 4 rings of gold, to make 4 legs for the table and put four rings in the four corners of the table. To make dishes and make spoons for the table and covers for the dishes, to make also bowels for the table. All the utensils are to be of pure gold and the showbread are to be set on the table always before God (Ex. 25:23-30).

The table vessels, dishes, bowels and spoons, were made of pure gold and were on the table for use in incense, meat and drink offerings and to hold the 12 loaves of bread which symbolized the 12 tribes of Israel as being in divine presence. There were to be 2 stacks of showbread placed on the table, each containing 6 flat loaves and these were to be exchanged for fresh loaves every Sabbath, incense was burned in a container placed on top loaf of each stack, signifying the worship of the 12 tribes (Levi. 24:5-9). The dishes were large receptacles in which the showbread was mixed, the spoons were small censers which incense was burned (Num. 7:14,20,26,32 etc). The bowels held blood of sacrifices and offerings (Ex. 37:16). The covers were large goblets or cups which held wine to be poured out before the Lord every Sabbath when the bread was changed. A cloth of blue cover was on the table on which all the loaves and utensils are

(Num. 4:7). The table was placed on the north side of the Holy tent opposite the lampstand. When the bread is changed, the bread of the previous week became food for Aaron and his sons. They were to eat it in the Holy place as an offering most holy of all the offerings of the Lord made by fire. (Lev. 24:5-9). While on travel a cover of scarlet and then another of badger skin covers the table and its vessels (Num. 4:8).

The table of the showbread is symbolic of the Messiah in his kingdom, the royal banquet table and the Messiah himself was both the table and the banquet. The shittim wood overlaid with gold signifies that this royal banquet in this divine presence is the same incorruptible son of man now totally overlaid in divinity, though he can never discard the human flesh that made him the son of man, his is totally back to the divine glory he had with the Father before the world was made. The blue cloth cover of the table shows that the table remains the same son of God represented in blue linen. The loaves of bread represents the body of Christ in the divine presence and the wine represents his blood shed to salvage creation. The gold crown and border round the table signifies that the table is royal and the banquet is of divine kingdom. The four rings in the four corners of the table are where staves are placed to carry the table on travel depicting that this table moves through the ends of the earth and with its four legs it stands firm in all the end of the earth. When on travel a cover of scarlet and another of badger skin shall be covered upon it and be carried by staves in the four rings. These signify that the Messiah unlimited in his spiritual mission moves around the whole world as a Savior (in scarlet), saving the world of all infirmities as he did among the Jews in his physical mission but the outer cover of badger skin depicts rejection. The pure gold dishes and spoons and bowels signify that this banquet is purely divine and that is why Paul asked us to understand what it means before we eat. The incense burnt upon the loaves represents the Messiah solicited for his body the church represented in the loaves.

We earlier said that whatever the spiritual mission of the Messiah is he achieves through his Church and whatever we explained here about the Messiah the same is his Church that is his body on earth. He confirmed himself as the table and the banquet when he says:

I am the living bread which came down from heaven: if any man eat of this bread, he shall live forever: and *the bread that I will give is my flesh, which I will give for the life of the world* (Jn. 6:51).

At the last super he established his church a table and banquet. The gospel according to Matthew put it this way:

And as they were eating, Jesus took bread,
and blessed it, and brake it, and gave it to the
disciples, and said, Take, eat; this is my body.
And he took the cup, and gave thanks, and gave it to
them, saying, Drink ye all of it; For this is my blood of the
new testament, which is shed for many for the remission
of sins (Matt. 26:26-28).

Paul explained further by saying:

For I have received of the Lord that which also I delivered
unto you, That the Lord Jesus the same night in which
he was betrayed took bread: And when he had given
thanks, he brake it, and said, Take, eat: this is my body,
which is broken for you: this do in remembrance of me.
After the same manner also he took the cup, when he
had supped, saying, this cup is the new testament in my
blood: this do ye, as oft as ye drink it, in remembrance
of me. For as often as ye eat this bread, and drink this
cup, ye do shew the Lord's death till he come. Wherefore,
my brethren, when ye come together to eat, tarry one for
another (1 Cor. 11:23-26, 33).

The Matthew text told us how Jesus instituted the table and the banquet but Paul in the next text explained clearly that the Lord instituted the church a table and banquet which shall be a continuous practice, a memorial of the Lord sacrifice till he retires. His last words that break the Carmel back is

"Wherefore, my brethren, when ye come together to eat, tarry one for another". The gathering of the Church is primarily for the banquet of the Lord and the church foundations in the four corners of the death are on the four legs of this table and because the outer cover of this table as it moves was of badger skin, it is the main part of the church life but is easily rejected.

In the last supper Jesus instituted the mystery between his sacrifice at Calvary and the table of showbread. As the Tabernacle expressed, it follows that after the Messiah has made the blood sacrifice and perfect the church in the Laver he entered the Holy place of heaven, his spiritual abode, and exchanged the old bread of sin and wickedness, and replaced them with the new and eternal bread of purity and truth, which is his body. He was to pour out the old wine of the old covenant and refill the goblets with the new and everlasting covenant in his blood. For what the bread and the meat meant for the Priests – he gave his body, and his blood he gave in place of wine and blood for the propitiation of the sin of the church. He made the church an eternal generation of Priests to eat of the meat, bread and drink offerings presented to God in the Church, which are now replaced with bread and wine.

The showbread represents comfort and satisfaction to the church through which the church perceives the presence of Christ in them (Jn. 14:18-21). The Holy Spirit the comforter receives from the table of showbread which is Jesus and gives comfort and satisfaction to the church (Jn. 16:14-15). Therefore, when the word of God or Jesus is preached in the presence of the Holy Spirit, signs and wonders follow (Mk. 16:20). The Holy Spirit confirms the presence of Jesus "the word" with signs following. No man therefore does signs and wonders but the Lord is the one who brings the showbread to comfort his people. The showbread is of sweet smell and bitter taste, owing to the frankincense used in consecrating the bread, having the smell and taste of frankincense itself. This expresses the sweet and bitter nourishment of Christian worship, the sweet nourishment of worthy worship and the bitterness of the unworthy worship, as Paul said about those that eat the body and blood of Christ unworthy (1 Cor. 11:27:30). The wine in the goblets represents strength for a worthy worshipper, the power of the Holy Spirit, but for the unworthy a gin and a snare and a stumbling block (Isa. 28:16, 8:14).

The showbread and wine also represents adversity and afflictions of the church (I mean bitter taste and sweet smell of the showbread and vinegar). Isaiah earlier before prophesied about the Lord and the church as depicted in the bread, its comfort and satisfaction, its bitter taste of adversity and affliction and sweet taste of inward joy of Holy Spirit directions and also the replenishing of the Lord after a while suffering (Isa. 30:18-26, 1 Pet. 5:10). The table was placed at the North side of the tent representing the heavenly mount Zion where the church is established in spiritual realm (Isa. 14:12- 14, Ps. 75:6-7, Heb. 12:22)

> *For the people shall dwell in Zion at Jerusalem: thou shall weep no more: he will be gracious unto thee at the voice of thy cry; when he shall hear, he will answer thee. And though the Lord give you the bread of adversity, and the water of affliction, yet shall not thy teachers be removed into a corner any more, but thine eyes shall see thy teachers. And thine ears shall hear a word behind thee, saying, this is the way, walk ye in it, when ye turn to the right hand, and when ye turn to the left. Ye shall defile also the covering of thy graven images of silver, and the ornament of thy molten images of gold: thou shalt cast them away as a monstrous cloth; thou shalt say unto it, get thee hence. Then shall he give the rain of they seed, that thou shalt sow the ground withal; and bread of the increase of the earth, and it shall be fat and plenteous. In that day shall thy cattle feed in large pastures (Isa 30:19-23).*

This spiritual mission of the Messiah in the table embodied more on the church dying with the Messiah, passing through adversity and afflictions in order to come to perfection. But no matter the gravity of such adversity and afflictions, inward joy of comfort will always be and as the church perfects they are replenished with good things. This Table of showbread is the strength of the spiritual adventure of the church, that is why Jesus instituted the physical symbol of the spiritual adventure and command that the church shall continue with symbol as often as possible.

2:5 GOLDEN ALTAR- Golden Altar of Incense

God commanded Moses to make an altar out of shittim wood, length 45cm, breadth 45cm, height 90cm attached with 4 corner projections and overlaid with pure gold. To put gold border round it, attach 2 gold rings below the 2 sides of the border for carrying it. To make poles of shittim wood covered with gold for the rings. To put the altar outside the curtains that hangs in front of the covenant box at the Westside of the Holy place forming a triangle with the lampstand and the table of showbread. At this altar God meets with Moses every time. Aaron comes in every morning and evening to make ready the lamp and burn sweet smelling incense on the altar, a steady and unperturbed offering. God commanded that he should not offer on it any forbidden incense or animal, grain or pour out any wine offering on it. Once in a year Aaron is to perform the rituals for purifying the altar by putting on it four projections the blood of animals sacrificed for sin, this altar is to be completely holy dedicated to the Lord (Ex 30:1-10).

The Golden altar of Incense like table of the showbread is symbolic of the Messiah in his kingdom, an altar and a place where God meets with man and the sweet incense of Man's worship ascends to God. The Messiah himself is both the altar and the incense, he represents in this place both Moses the mediator and Aaron the high priest performing the services of both for the redemption of mankind. We are aware that God meets with Moses every time to discuss the matters concerning His people Israel and Moses here mediate for them. Aaron would come in every morning and evening to burn sweet smelling incense on the altar, a steady and unperturbed offering and the Messiah is both the altar and the worship which signifies the incense. The shittim wood overlaid with gold signifies that this High Priest and Mediator in this divine presence is the same incorruptible son of man now totally overlaid in divinity. He is truly God and truly man because he cannot ever discard his human flesh but rather give way for the divine overlay of the human flesh of all who come to God through him.

I have earlier said that in this spiritual mission of the Messiah, whatever he represents is what the Church - his body - represents, and whatever represents him represents the Church. The Church, therefore, is the altar of worship, overlaid in divine. The golden altar represents the church in the holy presence of the Lord. Aaron and Moses are represented in the ministers of the Gospel of Christ and the burnt incense represents the prayer of the body of Christ - the Church - as it worships in divine presence. This area of the tent - the Golden altar of incense - is what was revealed to Apostle John when he says:

> *And another angel came and stood at the altar, having a golden censer; and there was given unto him much incense, that he should offer it with the prayers of all saints upon the golden altar which was before the throne. And the smoke of the incense, which came with the prayers of the saints, ascended up before God out of the angel's hand* (Rev. 8:3-4).

At this altar, once in a year, there are purification rituals which Aaron performs by putting on its four projections the blood of animals sacrificed for sin, the altar is completely holy dedicated to the Lord (Ex 30:1-10). The Messiah on his own part did the purification of the church once with his blood and dedicated it once and forever holy unto God. The Church of Christ stands continually in the presence of the Lord holy and fully dedicated to God. As we stand before the altar dedicated to God in our church buildings or in our homes we should know that the altar of the Most high God on earth represents the altar of incense in the holy presence of the Lord and Jesus Christ our mediator is that altar before God.

The gold crown and border round the altar as in the table of showbread signifies that that altar is royal and the priesthood is of divine kingdom. The four rings in the four corners of the altar are where staves are placed to carry the altar on travel depicting that this altar moves through the ends of the earth and with its four horns it projects to all the ends of the earth. When on travel a cover of scarlet and another of badger skin shall be covered upon it and be carried by staves in the four rings. These signify that the Messiah unlimited in his spiritual mission is the Royal High priest and the Saviour (in Scarlet) the whole world The altar is placed outside the curtains which hang in front of the covenant box as symbolic of Jesus as the curtain standing a gap between the spiritual and the divine to be an advocate between the church and God. As it was in this altar that Moses stood a gap to communicate with God to the affairs of the Israelites and Aaron officiated as Priest, the same way has the church become priests of the God to have access to God in worship while Christ stands as a mediator between God and the church.

Aaron coming every morning and evening to make ready the lamp and burn sweet smelling incense on the altar is symbolic of the continual worship of the church without ceasing and at worship the spirit of God kindles the hearts of the church to offer the fruits of their lips a holy sacrifice, holy and acceptable unto God. As the church continues unperturbed in worship the Holy Spirit lights continually the fire of God in them and strengthen them as they wait upon the Lord.
> ***And he spake a parable unto them to this end, that men ought always to pray, and not to faint*** (Lk. 18:1).

That Aaron should not offer forbidden incense or animal, grain or pour out any wine offering on it is symbolic of sanctified or spiritual worship of the church, devoid of animal instinct or quest for food and drink. For the church being dead with Christ is dead to the physical world with all its animal instincts and quest for materialism and careerism. Their worship was not to be in conformity to the world's standard as St. Paul rightly says:

> ***I BESEECH you therefore brethren, by the mercies of God, that ye present your bodies a living sacrifice, holy, acceptable unto God, which is your reasonable service. And be not conform to this world: but be ye transformed by the renewing of your mind, that ye may prove what is that good, and acceptable and perfect will of God*** (Rom. 12:1-2).

This altar being completely holy and dedicated to the Lord is symbolic of the church complete dedication to God in worship; rid of the world in their hearts, they continually worship their God in spirit and in truth, proving in their deeds what is that good and acceptable perfect will of God. This is the living sacrifice, acceptable at this altar, holy and dedicated unto God.

This altar of incense is strength in the spiritual adventure of the church with Christ the power behind the spiritual progress of the church. A prayerless Christian is a powerless Christian, therefore in worship the church shall continue without ceasing as they wait upon the Lord.

CHAPTER THREE

The Divine Second Advent of Messiah

3:1 **The Veil** – The curtain in front of covenant box

God commanded Moses to make a veil of fine linen woven with blue, purple and scarlet, embroided with figures of winged creatures, hang it on four posts of shittim wood covered with gold, fitted with hooks and set in four silver bases. To place the curtain under the row of hooks in the roof of the tent, and behind the curtain he should put the covenant Box containing the two stone tables. The veil (curtain) will separate the Holy tent from the most Holy tent (Ex. 26:31-33). The veil or the curtain in front of the Holy of Holies is symbolic of the Messiah interwoven personality as a prince with God and man that has prevailed as the son of God, Perfect man, King and Saviour, who is highly exalted and made beautiful like embroidered garment to stand as divine or eternal Lord and a mediator in God's covenants with man. A divine Lord to give divine and eternal inheritance to the redeemed men by bringing many redeemed sons and daughters unto divine nature and giving them authority to help in bringing many unto eternal inheritance.

The gold hook fitted on the post that held the veil on the posts signified the four divine ministrations of God's covenants back from the day of Adam to the eternal future as they fitly joined together the redeemed men of the covenants of God with man bringing them unto divine nature and inheritance enjoyable for 1000 years with Christ. The four shittim wood posts overlaid are symbolic of the Messiah's four arms of divine ministration given to mankind who were on special mission on earth, being redeemed by the blood of the Messiah, they stand before the throne of the Messiah upon the silver bases of redemption in bringing the redeemed men of God's covenants unto God (i.e. redeemed from the foundation of the earth). These four men represented in the four posts were given the power of the four angels of God's throne in different dispensations of God's covenants with man to work towards man's redemption on earth and before the throne they shall stand in the millennial reign of Christ.

> *And before the throne there was a sea of glass like unto crystal: and in the midst of the throne and round about the throne, were four beasts full of eyes before and behind. And the first beast was like a lion and the second beast like a calf, and the third beast had a face as a man, and the fourth beast was like a flying eagle. And the four beasts had each of them six wings about him: and they were full of eyes within: and they rest not day and night, saying Holy, holy, holy, Lord God Almighty which was, and is, and is to come* (Rev. 4:6- 8).

These beasts were always referred to as Angels, but as long as angel means messenger I can call them Angels but they are men. As long as the Tabernacle of Moses signified them as shittim wood posts overlaid with gold standing on silver bases, they are supposed to be incorruptible men made divine by the redemptive blood of Jesus, and the silver bases signified that they were redeemed. They are therefore men made divine princes to stand before the throne of the Messiah seeing over the affairs of his Divine kingdom or Divine reign. Being incorruptible signifies that they have corporeal ascension or translated body and soul before the millennium. Whenever the Bible speaks of beasts, the reference is to a man that is having the power of an angelic prince in order to have dominion over the earth. It may be either Angel of light or of darkness. In the Daniel Beasts of Dan. 7. The first beast like unto lion referred to Nebuchadnezzar having the power of the prince of Babylon. The second beast like bear was Astagyes king of Medo-Persia (Dan 9:11) having the power of the prince of Persia. (Dan. 10:20). The third was Alexander the great having that of the prince of the Grecian (Dan. 10:20). The forth was Pompey and decemvirate Roman Empire. The antichrists called beasts (Revelation 13:1-18 and 17:8-11) were men that will be having satanic authorities to be antichrists on earth.

With the above explanations, to refer the beasts of Revelation 4:6-8 and 5:8-10 as divine Angels is a contradiction to the other beasts, the only difference is that the others were having the powers of the satanic princes while these are having the powers of the Divine Angelic Princes of God. Isaiah also spoke about the beasts saying:

> *In the year that king Uzziah died I saw also the Lord sitting upon the throne, high and lifted up, and his train filled the temple. Above it stood the seraphims: each one had six wings; with twain he covered his face and with twain he covered his feet and with twain he did fly. And one cried unto another and said Holy, holy, is the Lord of hosts: the whole earth is full of his glory. And the posts of the door moved at the voice of him that cried, and the house was filled with smokes* (Isa. 6:1-4).

In this Isaiah's vision the Angelic beings were different from the posts but their powers were shaking the posts, it referred to these men when they were yet prophets of God on earth, the powers of the Angels were acting on them to accomplish their missions on earth, then they were not given dominions for they were yet prophets and servants of God but are full of mighty deeds. They were not destined to rule on earth but to minister words of salvation unto men. In the Divine reign of Messiah these men then redeemed by the blood of the Messiah shall assume the powers of these Angels to stand before the throne of Christ in millennium and be princes over the affairs of men and shall remain on the Messiah throne eternal after the restoration of all things.

The church is now under the spiritual reign of the Messiah but these topics we entered now speaks about the divine and eternal reign, all we are saying here shall be seen as to happen in the future when we shall see face to face with the Messiah both in millennium of divine reign and eternal. In this topic it expressed that in the divine reign of the millennium in the restored city of Jerusalem, the throne of the Messiah shall be on his temple and before his throne shall stand four redeemed men, having powers to rule and bring justice on earth. Then Jesus the Messiah shall be our divine Lord and king, our High Priest and mediator of the everlasting covenant the whole redeemed men shall be gathered together and be held together in one fold by the dominion of the four princes to form one people of God in one thousand years.

> *For unto us a child is born, unto us a son is given: and the government shall be upon his shoulder and his name shall be called Wonderful, Counselor, The Mighty God, The Everlasting Father, The Prince of peace. Of the increase of his government and peace there shall be no end, upon the throne of David upon his kingdom, to order it and to establish it with judgment and with justice from henceforth, even for ever. The zeal of the Lord of hosts will perform this* (Isa. 9:6-7).

This above quotation explained this topic expressing the interwoven personality of the Messiah in his Second Advent and his reign on earth. I said earlier on in this book that "unto us a child is born" referred Christ's humanity in his First Advent and "unto us a child is given" referred to his divinity and his Second Advent. In this Second Advent the interwoven personality of the Messiah shall be visible even his government and all things about him shall be made glorious like the embroidered veil of the sanctuary.

This divine reign will happen after the spiritual reign is over, after the rapture or the resurrection of the first fruits of the church. In the spiritual, the Messiah's kingdom is represented on earth by his church, but after the spiritual era, he will come to restore both the kingdom of David, the temple and the city of Jerusalem. He shall sit upon the throne of David as king over the entire humanity. With the four beasts on his throne having dominion to see that justice is done on earth. He shall in the temple also be the High Priest to stand a gap between God and man in the worship of the last and everlasting covenant. The raptured church that returned redeemed with him shall be priests of the temple in the sacrifices and ordinances of the divine covenant. The earth shall yet be in its natural state, with men going about their normal businesses. But the Jews who at this era have recognized their Messiah shall now go around the whole world to preach the presence of the Messiah in Jerusalem. So shall his government increase with peace following.

> *Of the increase of his government and peace*
> *there shall be no end, upon the throne of*
> *David and upon his kingdom* (Isa. 9:7).

In this reign, the four beasts of the throne shall have dominion over the earth to ascertain that justice is done. There shall be two types of humanity on earth then, the mortals and the immortals, all the resurrected saints that came back with Jesus shall be immortal beings while the rest of the mortals shall remain in their respective countries, going on pilgrimage to Jerusalem.

> *For I know their works and their thoughts: it shall come, that I will gather all nations and tongues and they shall come and see my glory. And I will set a sign among them, and I will send those that escape of them unto the nations, to Tarshish, Pul, and Lud, that draw the bow, to Tubal and Javan, to the Isels afar off, that have not heard of my fame, neither have seen my glory; and they shall declare my glory among the Gentiles. And they shall bring all your brethren for an offering unto the LORD out of all nations upon horses, and in chariots and in litters, and upon mules, and upon swift beasts, to my holy mountain Jerusalem saith the LORD, as the children of Israel bring an offering in a clean vessel unto the house of the LORD. And I will also take of them for priests and for Levites saith the Lord* (Isa. 66:18-21).

Immediately after the spiritual reign of the Messiah when the church has been raptured, comes great tribulation in Israel, many shall perish, many shall escape, and those that escaped or the remnant of Israel after tribulation shall Messiah send all over the world to preach his presence at Jerusalem. Then shall they also recognize that it was the same man they rejected and crucified, and then they shall mourn. The Messiah said earlier that happy are those that mourn for they shall be comforted.

> *And I will pour upon the house of David, and upon the inhabitants of Jerusalem, the spirit of grace and of supplications: and they shall look upon me whom they pierced, and they shall mourn for him, as one mourneth for his only son, and shall be in bitterness for him, as one that is in bitterness for him, as one that is in bitterness for his firstborn* (Zech. 12:10).

3:2 Ark of Covenant.

God commanded Moses to make an ark of shittim wood, with breadth 3ft 1½ in height 3ft 1½ in length 5ft 2½ in and overlay both inside and outside with pure gold. To make upon it a lid and crown of gold, cast 4 gold rings and put one in each corner. To make 2 staves of shittim wood overlaid with gold and put them into the rings on the sides of the ark which are not to be taken out. To put the testimony – 2 tables of stone, the 10 commandments – inside it and put the mercy seat above upon the ark (Ex 25:10-16, 21) The lid and crown of gold was removed from the ark and the ark was closed with mercy seat. The ark also has inside it the pot of manna, the bread from heaven, Israelis ate in the wilderness (Ex. 16:33, Heb. 9:4). Aaron's rod was placed on the ark as witness to Israel of God's choice of priesthood (Num. 17:10, Heb. 9:4) the ark is placed at the middle point just inside the veil. The high Priest goes before the ark to sprinkle blood only once in a year (Lev. 16, Heb. 9:3-7).

The ark of covenant is symbolic of the Messiah in his divine and eternal throne. He himself is the ark of the new and everlasting covenant God had with humanity and entire creation through man. He is our law of liberty, our bread of life and our shepherd, who has prevailed in his incorruptible flesh and was overlaid in divine glory, crowned to be our king eternal, our law giver, our source of life and our shepherd forever.

It represents also the divine presence that prepared, redeemed and made divine the incorruptible messengers of God's covenants, who are to be brought into divine reign of the Messiah. The elders to who God established His covenant in divers generations who are to serve the Messiah in his throne and reign with him through the millennium and forever. The Ark therefore the Messiah; the Lord of all God's covenants and the dispensational messengers of God's covenants before his eternal throne, who he made lawgivers with the law engraved in their heart and written in their mind. He has established them in his kingdom as a reward of their faithfulness to covenant they executed on earth in their different era. These elders are shepherds of different era commissioned and committed with a covenant of that era. They are signified in the Ark of Covenant as they are endowed with the divine nature of the Messiah, to serve and reign with the Great Shepherd and king forever. Over these shepherds were the throne of mercy established, for them being shepherds has the Messiah as their great shepherd and over Lord, in the presence of the throne. Before the angels of the throne and before Messiah shall they shepherd the saints while the Messiah stands a gap between them and God as a great advocate of humanity in matters of God's covenants with man. As the lid of the Ark was removed and it was covered with the Mercy seat, it signifies that these men of covenant were joined to make one piece with the Angels of the throne upon the mercy seat or throne of grace where the Messiah seats, and where they are to receive their crown as the fullness of their redemption.

> ***And round about the throne were four and twenty
> seats and upon the seats I saw four and twenty
> elders sitting clothed in white raiment; and they
> had on their heads crowns of gold*** (Rev. 4:4).

These elders are the men who received the covenant of God in all generation of men right from Adam, Noah, Abraham, Isaac, Jacob to mention but a few (but only God knows who). They are the hands that received the transfer of the scepter of covenants that God had with men, that is why they were represented in this Tabernacle with the ark of the covenant. In the Millennium of Messiah's divine reign on earth, these elders are to seat around his throne officiating in leadership and worships. They shall receive their crowns of glory that is now yet in the church, for each one of them has worked on earth in the establishment of God's covenants with humanity and the seals of these covenants with God brought many men of their time to perfection; they are therefore rewarded with divine nature and crown of glory to rule with the Messiah in his divine reign. In the throne of the Messiah, they shall reign for one thousand years and in the temple they shall sit as shepherds and priest to offer before the throne the fruits of the lips of all saints as a holy sacrifice acceptable to the Lord. All the prayers of the saints all over the earth are gathered in this throne as a sweet smelling sacrifice unto the Lord.

> And when he had taken the book, the four beast and four and twenty elders fell down before the Lamb, having every one of them harps, and go sung a new song, saying, Thou art worthy to take the book, and to ***open the seals thereof: for thou wast slain, and has redeemed us to God by thy blood out of every kindred, and tongue, and people and nation. And has made us unto our God kings and priests: and we shall reign on the earth*** (Rev. 5:8-10).

The everlasting covenant of God with man was under a seal that cannot be opened unless a son of man pays the price of redemption for man, though the 24 elders have covenants they received in their respective times yet none paid for man's redemption and were unworthy to open and read the new and everlasting covenant. It behooves only the Messiah who Jacobed mankind to open the book because it is only in his blood all are redeemed and eternal future is made possible for man. It was his blood that that gave hope and eternal gospel destiny for mankind. *"And has redeemed us by thy blood"* emphasized that there is no Angelic being that is involved in this worship, both the four beasts and twenty-four elders were redeemed men, who shall sit and stand around the throne of the Messiah in the Millennium, to serve him and work towards the redemption of the rest of the mortal humans on earth at that era, and also offer the sacrifice of the prayers of the saints on earth. Notice also the last words *"we shall reign on the earth" meaning* that this is a millennial reign on earth. These elders are to be princes and priests, reigning and collecting in golden veils the prayers that come as sweet smelling savours to the throne of the Messiah which are the prayers of the saints of the millennium. In the millennium the knowledge of prayer shall be well established in mankind for the laws of God shall then be fully imbibed in their heart as a living principle and in Messiah's throne the fruit of their lips shall be accepted as living sacrifice. Immediately the seal of the new covenant is opened on earth at millennium every heart that believed shall have its rules written in them.

> *But this shall be the covenant that I will make with house of Israel: after those days, saith the LORD, I will put my law in their inward parts and write it in their hearts: and will be their God, and they shall be my people. And they shall teach no more every man his brother, saying, know the LORD: for they shall all know me, from the least of them unto the greatest of them, saith the LORD: for I will forgive their iniquity, and will remember their sin no more (Jer. 31:33-34).*

The divine reign of the millennium shall be different from other dispensations, the law of Moses was of outward ordinances, everyday observation of ordinances and in spiritual dispensation it was evangelism all the way; like Paul plants, Apollos waters and God brings the increase but in the divine reign there should not be any labour of planting and watering the words of God's covenant in humanity the only job is to inform men that the kingdom has come. And as long as Satan shall be bound for those 1000 years, evil shall not therefore exist but whoever deliberately sins shall be executed to eternal death. The four beasts of the throne are full of eyes to monitor (Rev. 4:6) all the activities of humanity in the millennium and as long as it behooves them to execute judgment upon humanity in that era, no matter the fact that all men shall live without dying then, they still have the divine authority to put to death any rebellious man. Being full of eyes, no man can escape their monitory eyes. The whole sacrifice of prayers shall then be sweet smelling savour before the Lord, therefore whoever that mixed it up with bad odour of a sinner's prayer shall be detected by the beasts who will equally put such person to death. Remember that we shall have this earth then as it is now except Jerusalem that will inhabit immortal saints, which the Messiah shall restore to a divine glory and the rest of humans the lives in all ends of the earth shall be coming to Jerusalem for pilgrimage, kings and nations shall be coming to resolve their differences before him that is greater than Solomon.

> *And it shall come to pass, when ye be multiplied and increased in the land, in those days, saith the LORD, they shall say no more, the ark of the covenant of the LORD: neither shall it come to mind: neither shall they remember it; neither shall they visit it; neither shall that be done any more. At that time, they shall call Jerusalem the throne of the LORD; and all the nations shall be gathered unto it, to the name of the LORD, to Jerusalem: neither shall they walk any more after*

the imagination of their evil heart (Jer. 3:16-17).

3:3 The 4 coverings of the Holy tents

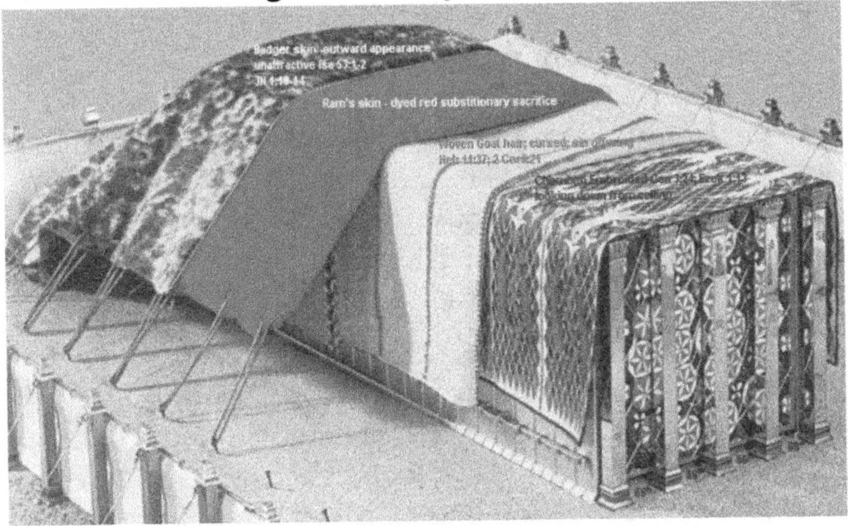

1.   The under material of fine linen curtains housed the holy place and the most holy place or Holy of holies. It is the same as the fence curtain, the world outside the church see in it the perfect man and that is all they know about Christ, the church and the saints or the members of the house hold of God which the house represents.

2.   The next or first roof inner covering was of goat hair that represents the prophet and can only be seen by those inside the tents. To the outside world, because they cannot enter nor see the roof, they see the prophecy of the Messiah and the church as mombo jombo, for this reason therefore they are suspicious of men that are led by the Spirit of God. They doubt the power of Christ and attribute the works to Satan. The only thing they expect of a Christian it to appear perfect in all things. Any other thing beyond that is not of Christ. Jesus earlier said:

> *It is enough for the disciple that he be as his master, and the servant as his lord. If they have called the master of the house Beelzebub, how much more shall they call them of his household?* (Matt. 10:25).

3.   The next or first outer covering was of ram skins dyed red. This cover is neither seen by those inside nor outside, it is the mystery of redemption of the entire creation and can hardly be understood unless by the Holy Spirit revelation. This is the hardest things for the world outside the church to believe; that a man shed his blood for another to be redeemed and also the hardest part of spiritual sacrifice that discourage those that would be Christian; risking your life for the sake of another or loving your enemies.

4.   The last or the most outside covering was of badger skins to withstand weather. This is the cover most men outside the church see about the Messiah, they expected a Christian to always look rejected, smile in the face of every hardship and accept every persecution with endurance. To prophesy is mombo jombo and to risk your life in defence of others is foolishness. But all these are part of the Church spiritual adventure with Christ, which the world outside can never understand and will always reject Christ and Christians to that effect. What exactly are they rejecting? They are actually rejecting their outer cover that offered them protection and at the same time reject all that is inside the made them perfect, guide them to their eternal destiny and give them life.

These coverings represent the shadows of Messiah covering the church in all era both the spiritual and divine era and a Messiah coverage to all men in the millennium. The housing of fine linen signifies the Messiah as a perfect man and God's eternal purpose that he shall bring all men to perfection by his blood even as many as believed in him. In goat hair, we see the Messiah as a prophet in whom all the church shall be prophetic in his spiritual reign and the whole humanity in his divine or millennial reign. Reference to the restoration of the kingdom of Jerusalem unto the Messiah for his divine reign and the ushering in of the whole humanity into this tents of the Lord's presence, God says:

> *And it shall come to pass afterward, that I will pour out my spirit upon all flesh; and your sons and your daughters shall prophecy, your old men shall dream dreams, your young men shall see visions: and also upon the servants and upon the handmaids in those days will I pour out my spirit* (Joel 2:28-29).

These prophets' shadows of the Messiah in goat hair housed both the Holy place and the holy of holies signifying this prophecy to fulfil in both the spiritual and divine reign of the Messiah. It is already fulfilling in the church (Act 2:16-21) at this spiritual reign but yet in his divine reign the Spirit shall come upon all flesh as a renewed era of humanity on earth. When God created man, he had never wanted man to serve him with human abilities, the moment he breathed into man, he wanted His Spirit to be in man so that man can be able to say yes to his will at all time. And that is the Spirit our father Adam lost at Eden. But God eternal will has purposed that man in the Church of Christ should enjoy again this privilege in the spiritual reign of Messiah and the entire remnants of humanity in the divine reign of Messiah.

In ram's skin dyed red, the Messiah was symbolized as the lamb that was slain, the most effective self-sacrifice ever known through which those who learnt self-sacrifice attains unto redemption to live and reign with him in Millennium and eternal. The cup of sacrifice is the one of intimacy with God. Therefore, whoever that learns temperance through suffering shall be worthy of the millennial and eternal reign, and all men shall in those days be sacrificial to the divine reign; both them that have received dominion and all the ends of the earth where the spirit of God rests upon men.

Badger skins are symbolic of the Messiah who in his sacrifice considered not the beauty of his skin. He prefer the dignity of himself, the redemption of man and the restoration of man back to the dignity of Eden. The flesh, its laxity and desires was, not able to hinder his mission. It signifies also that flesh and self, have no part in the Church during the spiritual era and the whole humanity on divine era. The beauty of the flesh shall be of no value then, but the divine inheritance shall be.

The badger skin also signifies that all the stones that are bedrocks of spiritual and divine reign of the Messiah are all rejected stones; men that are regarded of no value while they were on earth. Then the riches of the world shall crumble while the poor and the outcast shall reign with the Messiah. And they that shall be rewarded then are those with broken spirit, penitent spirit, mild temper or gentle spirit, hungering and thirsting spirit for righteousness, compassionate and merciful spirit, pure spirit, spirit of wisdom and mediation, longsuffering and forgiving spirit (Matt 5:1-12).

The above are the spirits of Christ, expected that men with such spirit shall reign with the Messiah in the millennium.

3:4 The Mercy Seat : Eternal Reign of The Messiah

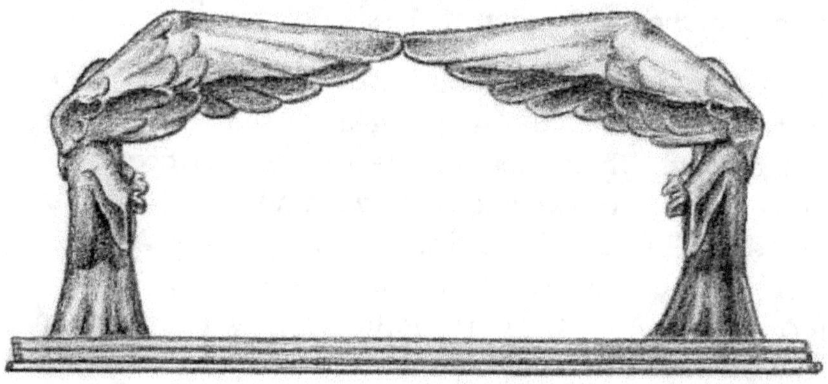

God commanded Moses to make a mercy seat of pure gold. To

make at the two ends of the mercy seat 2 cherubim made of beaten gold with their wings stretched forth high, covering mercy seat and with their faces looking towards each other. And to put the mercy seat on top of the ark (Ex. 25:17-21). The continual incense ascends up before the mercy seat from which the Lord was to speak to his people and bless or curse them as they would obey or disobey the covenant. The mercy seat was symbolic of the Judgment throne of Messiah; it was made entirely with pure gold to signify the throne as purely divine. The cherubims are also made of hammered gold to show that they are purely divine angels of judgment. When the Messiah might have ruled with redeemed men on earth for one thousand years, he shall ascend to heaven, and then Satan shall be loosed again who will gather great number of men out of the living mortals to besiege the city of the immortal saints. Then shall the great angels of the judgment throne come and put the Satan's existence to an end and usher in the throne of judgment (Rev. 20:7-11). The Messiah shall then come upon the throne, on his appearing shall the heaven and earth fold away and all the dead shall rise and appear before the throne, the righteous whose names are found in the book of life shall be ushered into eternal life while those that are not found in the book of life or those whose names are in the book of death shall be condemned to eternal death in hell fire along with Satan and all the antichrist. (Rev. 20:11-15, Dan. 12)

After these shall a new heaven and earth appear where there will be no more sea. (Rev. 21:1-2; Pet. 3:13) and a holy city of Jerusalem with courts like the Tabernacle shall descend from heaven where all the saints shall dwell forever. The throne of Christ as was depicted in the mercy seat upon the covenant box, shall be in the Tabernacle above all dominions, principalities and powers while God himself will be all in all and the light of his glory shall be light for the city, where there shall be no more night. In the new city of Jerusalem there shall be the Holy of holies where there shall be the throne of Christ above the thrones of the 24 elders. The holy tent of the Lord's presence shall house the first resurrected and raptured saints while the outer court shall be for

ABOUT THE AUTHOR

 The Author, Captain (Dr.) Igwebuike Okoye Ph.D, FICSM, CMILT, ACIS, MISMON, is a retired Naval Captain, a Corp Commander and the zonal Director of special duties, South/south zonal command of Nigerian Legion Corps of Commissionaire. He is one of the Senior Executive Officers of World Christian Crusade Centre in Nigeria and the author of Consider the Lilies.

The fundamentals of the Holy Oracles is an inquiry into the Oracles (The Tabernacle) of God which God commanded Moses to build in the wilderness. The explanations in this book suggested that God used the Oracles as mode of communication not because he would that man should sacrifice animals to Him but to make meanings and convey His mind to human race so that through the semiotics a logical mind with the help of the Holy Spirit, will understand the mind of God. Igwebuike Okoye has explicitly made know the meaning of the Oracles, the languages of the Oracles, the pedagogy and the andragogy of the Oracles. Fundamentals of the Holy Oracles is a great insight to who Christ is, why he came to the earth, why he died and resurrected, how and why he should return to the earth. It is a great piece of writing that can edify and enable a Christian stand up on his or her faith and confess Christ any time anywhere.

www.ingramcontent.com/pod-product-compliance
Lightning Source LLC
Chambersburg PA
CBHW060100260726
48658CB00004B/1349